ANGELS GUIDE

The Spiritual Toolbox for Using Angelic Guidance in Everyday Life

Belinda Womack

ANGELS GUIDE BOOKS

Published by Angels Guide Books
A Division of Angels Guide Inc.
P.O. Box 260, Tappan, NY 10983-0260
http://www.angelsguide.com

Robert Davidson, Executive Producer and Composer of Angels Guide Music
Daniel Cowett, Composer of Angel Messages music
Book Design: LaBreacht Design, Cindy LaBreacht
Jacket and Web site art: Gloria Petron
Marvyn W. Blair, Editor
Audio CD Digitally recorded and mastered at Fairbanks Sound, New York

Printed in the United States of America.

Library of Congress Catalog Card Number 97-74464
ISBN: 0-9659850-0-8

First Edition

For the acknowledgement of

his miraculous ability to bring to life

God's Child in everyone he meets.

Thank God for you, Jack W. Womack

Message from the Author

I was born with the ability to communicate with my Friends, the Twelve Archangel Kingdoms of the Central Soul (Sun). Although They have always been with me, I confess I abandoned Them when I was 12. It wasn't until I was working as a research biologist six years ago, that we were reconnected. My dear friend Liz decided I could do with some inner child therapy and sent me to her friend, Tom Kenyon. Using his amazing toning gifts, he magically readjusted my brain and reopened my clairvoyant vision. There I was surrounded by 12 incredibly bright Angels all singing to me.

The Twelve Archangels have guided me through my own healing and reuniting with my God Self. I have used the same Tools They use on me to help my many courageous clients break free from fear and unworthiness. I have conducted private and family Angel therapy sessions, and taught classes on the Archangels' teachings for the past five and a half years.

Angels Guide is my first book co-created with the Angels. All the material in Angels Guide is Truth and as the Angels will tell you, Their Tools come with a 100 percent guarantee. It works!

The Twelve Archangels of the Central Soul send Their gratitude in abundance to Robert Davidson, Executive Producer, and Composer of Angels Guide Music and to Daniel Cowett, Composer of music for the Angel Messages.

Belinda Womack and Robert Davidson are forever grateful to our benefactors, friends and families for assiting us in manifesting on Earth as it is in Heaven, the Angels Guide Book and Audio CD.

CONTENTS

ANGEL TREASURY

ANGEL LETTERS

USING ANGELS GUIDE

ANGELS GUIDE, the book, is divided into four parts for easy daily reference and reflection: Angel Messages, Angel Treasury of Six Books, Angel Letters, and the Angel Glossary.

ANGEL MESSAGES section can be read for daily guidance by simply closing your eyes and opening the first part of the book. Each message includes a short imagery exercise to help you integrate the message into your conscious reality.

ANGEL TREASURY supplies you with all the background information, guidance, and techniques for spiritual Self-help in breaking free from fear, abandonment, unworthiness, poverty, illness, and victim-consciousness. Simple imagery exercises using the Angel Fires and affirmations can be used at any time, anywhere.

ANGEL LETTERS give special instruction on the art of: telepathic communication between people, experiencing Angels with your young children and teens, crisis management tools for both individuals and counselors, and an Angel home remedy to help in the recovery from depression.

THE GLOSSARY is designed to assist the reader on fully understanding the words and concepts used by the Twelve Archangels. The Angels invite you to stroll through the glossary when seeking a quick boost of Angel inspiration or insight.

THE AUDIO CD allows the reader to fully experience God's healing Energy delivered by the Twelve Archangels of the Central Soul. It presents a sampling of four messages recorded with music: Message 1, The Holy Spirit; Message 8, How to Love a Human Being; Message 15, Facing Your Shadow Self; and Message 36, The Law of Attraction. The audio CD includes a recording of Book One of the Angel Treasury (with music), several of the imagery exercises for Books Two, Three and Five, Letter on Depression and Pain, and the entire meditation "Rainbow Soul" channeled by the Archangels to facilitate the integration of all six books of the Angel Treasury.

SOUNDTRACK (available 8/21/98) The soundtrack presents the instrumental versions of the Angel Treasury and Meditations audio recordings.

ANGELS GUIDE AUDIOBOOKS (available 8/21/98) contain the complete 36 Angel Messages and the six books of the Angel Treasury plus the four Angel Letters all recorded with original music.

ANGELS GUIDE MEDITATIONS (available 10/21/98) is a set of six guided imagery meditative journeys not in print in any of the other products. The meditations were created to assist with the cellular integration of the material presented in the six books of the Angel Treasury.

ANGELS GUIDE CD-ROM (to be released 10/20/98) is designed to bring the words, music and Angel Fires to life. Here you can experience more Angelic Guidance in a beautifully illustrated interactive setting. The Angels Guide CD-ROM is different each time you use it.

The CD-ROM has all the guided imagery of all 36 Angel Messages recorded with original music and read by the author. Each day a new imagery exercise for the day is selected for each user.

An "Angels Guidance" section allows you to select from a wide variety of different subjects on everyday issues and receive specific guidance in "Gabriel's Book of Love." When you have finished reading Gabriel's message, you are escorted to the magical Angel Power Tool treasure chest where the Angel Fire you need can be discovered and experienced.

The Twelve Archangels want you to understand Their words of wisdom as well as experience Their healing music and dazzling colors of the Angel Power Tools. The CD-ROM compliments the written book and audio CD and provides additional delightful experiences for you to begin and end your day.

The book with audio CD, the Angels Guide Soundtrack, the Messages and the Treasury audiobooks, the Meditations CD/cassette and the CD-ROM have been co-created with Archangel magic so they can be enjoyed again and again. With each exposure to Angels Guide, the participant can receive new insights at ever-increasing depths of awareness of where they have been and where they are going.

Angels Guide offers a complete Self-help toolbox guiding humans on their evolutionary journey home to a truly Divine state of living.

Enjoy!

For more information on Angel Guide products visit the web site at www.angelsguide.com. or call 1-800-525-4274.

Angel Messages

MESSAGE 1

The Holy Spirit

Today We remind you to breathe, to breathe in deeply and exhale slowly. Angels live forever because their food is Holy Breath, love, and music. We offer this nourishment to you in great abundance. Feast on Holy Breath by remembering to breathe as Angels do, deeply filling Ourselves with Holy Spirit, Divine Essence of Mother God. The air you breathe, no matter how polluted your scientists report it to be, is filled with Holy Spirit. Mother God's Energy stays fresh and pure because this is Her way of feeding Her sweet Children of Earth.

Magic happens when you remember with each breath you inhale, you are bringing in Mother God's Love into every atom, thought, feeling, and sense of your Self. Awareness of what you are really doing when you breathe will make a profound difference in your life. When you are aware of Holy Spirit, fear melts away, as does disharmony, disease, and depression. We wish to add that if you discover you are forgetting to breathe, fear has entered or surfaced from somewhere inside. Whisper the word *Angel*, or the word *God,* and We will come and remind you to breathe in deeply and exhale slowly, breathing as a happy, free Child of God.

Close your eyes, and begin to breathe slowly and deeply. Imagine you are resting on a ruby pink cloud of Light. Invite Mother God to love you, to hold you, rock you, and feed you at Her breast. Visualize Her pink Light of purest Love saturating your entire Self inside, outside, and all around you. Whisper the words "I love you" to the little child inside you.

We love you and wish you a joyous day.

Message 1 is included on the audio CD.

MESSAGE 2

CREATIVITY

Each individual soul expresses the creative force of God in a unique manner. When the creative door of the soul is opened, God's voice begins to flow from your very own Divine music box. When you listen to this magnificent music, life can become a miraculous manifestation of the highest ideals of your mind and purest desires of your heart.

Fear causes the lid to catch on its hinges, and fear creates whining noises when the key is first wound. Fear confuses the ears so you may question, "Is this truly God's voice I hear?" We wish to help you remember how to open your sacred music box and dust the fears away.

We are here to show you how to ignite the creative force of your soul again and again until you are prosperous, filled with purpose, and living your greatest potential. Join Us, and raise your soul's voice in God's song of everlasting joy.

Begin to breathe in a lovely golden Light. Bring the Light all the way to your toes, and when you exhale, see the gold Light gently swirl all around you. Say inside to yourself the words, "I Am opening," three times, and see the gold Light sparkle like flakes of gold metal in the sun. Allow yourself to dissolve into sparkles, and then take a great deep breath and imagine you explode in an infinite fiery Light and proclaim inside, "Yes, I Am the creative expression of God!" To fully feel this sacred dance, repeat the process two more times.

MESSAGE 3

SURRENDER

During times of stress, humans ask Us if God has any understanding for humanity's misery and desperation. Through your life lessons and human suffering, you are challenged to discover the indestructible God fiber within you. Your greatest moments of hopelessness are also your deepest moments of surrender. Surrender brings you awareness and insight into your truth, and it is through total surrender to Mother Father God within you and all around you that the greatest miracles happen.

Total surrender is about taking a deep breath and stopping the mind, letting go of control, and believing in the mercy and Divine wisdom of your God Self. In these moments where you are willing to give up everything you believe you know, We see you expand the most.

Expansion of your faith will set you free from physical, emotional, and mental prisons so that you are ready to believe life is worth living again.

We now present you with a recipe for surrender. The Angelic kingdoms responsible for the healing of Earth and the Master Buddha co-created a magical resting spot for suffering humans to voice their frustrations to Mother Father God. Buddha and the Angels call this sacred place the Golden Light Pity Pot. The pity pot is accessible through your desire and imagination, and all who are sad and feeling hopeless are welcome to come and profess their hurts to Beings of Light.

Come and allow your broken self to totally surrender to Mother Father God's compassion. Simply close your eyes and say inside, "I Am surrender." Golden Angels will come and bring you to the pity pot. We welcome you to bare your heart and tell Us your troubles. Breathe in the Light, and exhale the discontentment. Open to the Light, and as you open your heart, your mind will open as well. Miracles come in abundance, ah sweet surrender.

Yes, We promise to assist you, dear Child of God!

MESSAGE 4

TRANSFORMATION

Humans have been conditioned to believe that seeing is believing. What you can see, feel, touch, taste, and hear constitutes what is reality because you perceive your outer world as finite, solid, and slow to change. Human reality is more like a movie, an illusionary documentary filled with passionate drama. The dramas in your life's movie are seductive and consuming, and sometimes We see you believing drama is all there is. Angels and Guides and other assorted Beings of Light hope to help you untangle yourselves from the great spiderwebs of human drama by reminding you to edit your documentary anytime you choose.

Life's movie feels like permanent reality when humanity forgets Earth is a schoolroom designed to show you where you are still separate from your heart, your will, and your confidence. It is Our deepest desire to once again show you, as Children of God, you always have choice; no matter how unchangeable life's situations seem to you, a whole new world of experiences awaits you each time you challenge your fears and break through the illusion of your attachments.

Often, your past experiences flavor your aspirations for tomorrow. We will teach you how to transform these past experiences so you need not carry them into your future. We will show you how to transform your fears into love, and quickly your drama will become a comedy of illusions. Come and allow Us to show you the way out of the wilderness of your attachments, broken dreams, and impossibility. Let Us walk with you into your new reality of conscious choice and conscious freedom. Make a new movie with scenes overflowing with hope, joy, and richest experience.

Close your eyes, and imagine you are walking into a beautiful green forest. The branches of the trees knit together over your head, creating a magical tunnel. Walk under the trees, and see the green change to a brilliant violet. The violet Light is the Angel Fire of Transformation and Forgiveness. As you walk under the violet

canopy, imagine a gentle violet Light-colored rain beginning to fall from far above you. Walk in the gentle rain, breathing in the Transformation and Forgiveness, and know this Energy of God is transforming into love your fears, regrets over your past, and anxieties concerning your future. Love will set you free and put you on a new path to everlasting joy.

Stay in the violet Light as long as you like, walking in the purple forest with the rain washing all the drama away. Say inside the words, "I Am FREE!" Angel energy is magical and miraculous, and so We invite you to visit this experience often. The more frequently you partake of the Kingdom of God, the faster you see results in your daily life.

MESSAGE 5

COMING HOME

On the days that the analytical mind demands control, the Ego Self releases with full force the judging, comparing, and wanting torpedoes. These torpedoes are thoughts that explode in your head, demanding that you must know what is going to happen next. Before you take your next breath, your thoughts are racing down Scenario Lane, searching for the right house where you can hide safely and prepare yourself for all the worst that can happen.

The Ego is the part of your mind that identifies itself as separate from God and Creation. It holds within it your personality and how you see yourself in your outer world. The Ego mind has great potential for leading you away from your Center, that intuitive all-knowing space where you feel kindred with the universe.

When you are thinking from your Center, your head and heart are connected to your inner voice. This voice of God within you has all the answers to all the questions, and when you obey this voice, you are always living your life for your highest joy and good. When you live life from your Center, a calm, peaceful, and confident feeling radiates out from your whole Self. In this place, you are home and focused on the moment. The Center has no room for fear because you are moving with the flow of God, and everything is in place for you.

In truth, your Ego was designed to bring you back home to the heart of Spirit. We desire to show you how to integrate your Ego Self, your beautiful, questioning human personality, with your Center, the home of God within you. As the Ego and Center become united again, you will discover the tremendous power of staying present and in tune with all of the Cosmos.

To open and expand the Center of God within you, the umbilical chord of Christ/Buddha Light of Divine Love must be connected from your heart to the heart of Mother Father God. We ask you to breathe in deeply and exhale slowly. Imagine you are standing under a brilliant white golden Light. See your Self stretching up

to greet the Light, and allow the Light of Divine Love to flow into your head and travel all the way down into your feet. The white golden Light is now pouring in, completely filling you until it overflows out through every pore of your body. It even flows out through the soles of your feet and palms of your hands.

Gently, with deep slow breaths, allow your Self to totally dissolve in the Love. Quietly say inside, "I Am home, Ego come home with me" again and again until you feel relaxed, clear, and peaceful all over.

MESSAGE 6

DIVINE ORDER

Every event in the Cosmos, seen and unseen, is perfectly orchestrated by the Will of Mother Father God. Divine Will, or Divine Order, is the highest form of government for humanity, and no earthly laws can negate Mother Father God's Will. When you consciously choose to obey God's Will by listening to the voice of God within you, you will know and trust that each and every experience in your life happens for the greatest good of all concerned.

Often, it is difficult for humans to know their Truth, and yet all that is needed is a sincere intention to listen to your God Self. Divine Order will miraculously choreograph life's lessons until you see, feel, l trust your Truth and understand how to live your Divine Will right here on Earth.

Mother Father God within you and all around you supports every moment of your life with unconditional Love. Every Child of God has a Divine Destiny, a purpose for being here and as you learn to have faith again in Divine Order, you break free from believing you are a victim of circumstance or a victim of your past. It is God's Will for you to live life free from fear and fear's entrapment of separation from Oneness.

Ask to know God's Will in the decisions you make in your daily life, and ask to understand the Divine Order in your past experiences. Your path home to living in Heaven here on Earth will be Lighted with Truth, and you will know what actions to carry out for the greatest good of all.

We introduce you to Archangel Michael, Angel of the Lord. The word "Lord" means the Will of God. Michael's energy protects the Truth and establishes God's Law and Order here on Earth. Begin by closing your eyes and placing your right hand on your heart, with your fingers touching your throat. Visualize a lovely

sapphire-blue color, God's Light of Will and Truth, flowing into your throat and into your heart. Know Michael's Fire is burning through any obstacles to Truth in your mental, emotional, physical, and spiritual body. As Michael fills you with Will, see the Light become a great sapphire-blue ocean, and you are a dolphin or a whale swimming in Divine Purpose, Destiny, Freedom, and Truth.

And as you swim in the great Ocean, say inside the words, "I Am the Will of God" over and over and know that your Will blazes out as a great blue flame of Light for all the world to see.

MESSAGE 7

Listening to your intuition

Your all-knowing intuitive Truth lives deep inside your thinking mind and speaks out to you constantly, no matter where you are or what you are doing. This well of guidance is available to you when you remember to listen, to listen without talking. Thoughts are very talkative, and often they compete for your attention. It can be quite challenging to distinguish between the soft and subtle intuition and the boisterous, non-stop chatter of conscious thoughts.

Conscious thoughts are like a committee of experts who give you a list of tasks you need to do and at the same time offer suggestions on how to avoid doing the tasks for a little longer. Listening to these experts may seem like listening to a room filled with supervisors ordering you here and there, pointing out what you are not doing fast enough or well enough.

In contrast, intuitive thoughts are gently whispering all the answers to all your questions and pointing you to your Truth, the path of least resistance, the direction for the highest joy and good of all. Your intuition always knows the easy way of doing everything you need and want to do. Intuition allows your heart and mind to connect and your body to be calm and centered.

We are here to teach you how to experience these amazing thoughts of clear insight and total uncompromisable Truth 24 hours a day. The practice begins with taking a steady and deep inhale and then exhaling completely. Focus your attention on listening by sweeping aside any thoughts traveling through your mind, an experience similar to tuning out the voice of a boring lecturer. Politely escort out any memories arising from the past or thoughts of the future. Allow your awareness to drift as if in a daydream into the blank space you have just created and ask a question. Any question will do, and one We recommend you ask is, "What is my purpose here on Earth?"

You may also wish to ask the question, "What do I need to do for the greatest benefit of all concerned today?" The intuitive voice is infinite, all-knowing, and perfect in its accuracy. The more you listen to your intuition, the louder and more distinguished it becomes. Eventually, the experts of the conscious mind will be quiet and follow the directions given by the voice of God within you.

We present you with a way to silence all the confusing, loud, and busy thoughts and engage your intuition. Begin to breathe in deeply and exhale slowly. Focus all of your attention on your spinal column, all the way from your head down to your sacrum. Try to feel your whole spine at the same moment. Imagine the brilliant white Light of Divine Love flowing into the top of your head and pouring down your spine, and feel your entire spine melt like a stick of butter in the warm sun. Keep breathing and melting and listen, just listen and ask a question. Listen and Breathe and Melt and Know.

How to Love a Human Being

We have discovered how very little humans understand about loving humans. Human beings have three basic requirements for survival: affection, attention, and acknowledgment. Being a most miraculous invention of God, you are composed of love, and the more you remember how to love your whole Self — your mental, emotional, physical, and spiritual bodies — the faster you create your happiest dreams-come-true.

In every adult human lives a Child of God wanting to experience the miracle of unconditional love. You can begin to learn how to love this child inside you by practicing unconditional loving on your family, friends, co-workers, enemies, and strangers.

Angelic Beings love only unconditionally, and so We present you with how We love you. First, Angels love humans by giving them all the space they need to learn their lessons. We have no expectations for your behavior because We understand you are behaving just as you need to. We do not judge you or question your judgments, nor do We compare you to any other human, for We know you are the only one like you. It is impossible for you to be just like anyone else, and as all Children of God are created from Divine Love, inequality simply does not exist. The most important thing about how Angels love is that We have no expectations for how or when or where you are supposed to love us back.

The Great Expectation your Divine Mother Father has for you is that you will choose to love yourself unconditionally, follow your heart's desires, and live on Earth as you do in Heaven.

When you love someone, the love will always come back to you, but not always in the way you expect. Humans spend a great deal of time trying to define the nature of their relationships, and We tell you all of your relationships are Family relationships. Each human being wants to be loved and respected and feel important enough to you to receive your focused attention, affection, encouragement, and appreciation. Allow the love you give to each member of your Family to return to you in its own time and own way.

Surrender your expectations, open your heart, and Love One Another. Love given as a gift without strings attached will multiply and flow back to you in joyful abundance.

Close your eyes, and see your Self enter the door of your heart. Inside, you will find a little child wanting to receive your love and affection. Scoop this beautiful being of Light up in your arms, and together walk to a pool filled with pink Light, the Light of unconditional Love. Together, jump into the pool, and turn on the Jacuzzi jets. Laugh and play and splash in the pink bubbles. Soak up the Light until you both feel completely pink through and through. Enjoy the feeling of pure Love, given and received so freely. True Love is all there is. And Love, Love, Love is all a human needs.

Message 8 is included on the audio CD.

MESSAGE 9

IMAGINATION

Imagination is the window through which seers, prophets, and clairvoyants receive visions from God. This window can work like a tunnel or doorway linking the human mind to the inner planes, the dimensions beyond what is here on Earth. Imagination creates images from thought; therefore, for a human being to receive accurate images untouched by fear and by the Ego mind's control, it is always wise to ask to see only what is for the greatest good and highest truth for Oneness.

Angels believe that now is the time for all of humanity to remember how to send messages to God through images. When you link the creative force of the imagination with your intuition, God's voice within you, you open up a source of miraculous creative power.

We ask you to clear your mind of all negative thoughts and impressions. Think of a miraculous experience you wish to have happen for yourself or someone you love. Picture the experience with your imagination, and then send the image to Us. The vision of the desired experience is then presented to your OverSoul, the part of you never separated from Oneness. Your miracle will manifest in the time and manner for your highest joy and good, and often you experience something even better than what you asked for.

Start each day with imagining, sending images to God, of all you would like to experience. Imagine you are living a brand new life in total freedom and joy here on Earth. Help Us to help you create your heart's desires and make them come true!

Now We wish to present you with an easy way to receive clairvoyant visions from God.

Close your eyes, and image you are wearing a bright violet bike helmet on your head. The bike helmet is an image that activates the Violet Fire, God's Energy of Transformation, in your own crown chakra. This energy works like a filter to filter out all fearful thought so you can send and receive images of Truth.

Breathe in slowly, exhale completely, and continue to picture the Violet Fire bike helmet. When your mind feels free, imagine a beautiful place where you would love to take a vacation. Imagine you are resting in complete peace and serenity, and then ask your Angels to show you a vision concerning you, an insight you have been waiting for.

We remind you of a basic truth: Your past is gone, and your future is not here yet. If you ask to see your future, be open to something even better. If you see visions of your future, understand We often speak to you in symbols. Keep looking through the window, and the window becomes the door. Understanding will come. Trust what you see, follow your heart, and know at all times that only your greatest good can come to you.

Gratitude

Human Beings have the Divine Destiny to live on Earth in complete freedom and harmony. It is your birthright to have all the money, material resources, loving relationships, good health, and inspiring work your heart needs and wants.

The fastest way to jump over fear's obstacles of poverty of spirit, mind and body is to practice Gratitude. Gratitude is about giving thanks for everything you experience and taking the time to allow these experiences to show you where you are still buying into fear's illusions. Because your planet is a schoolroom, you can use the power of Gratitude to learn what you need to learn from separation and move on to living a heavenly life right in your own living room.

Gratitude brings a magical energy that is peaceful and brings a new perspective into dying and impossible situations. Giving thanks and trusting that each and every lesson is for your greatest good melts the resistance of the Ego Self and sends the Shadow Self running. The Shadow Self is the voice inside that tries to sabotage your faith in your Self and in God.

Gratitude will catapult you out of nearly every stagnant situation you find yourself trapped in. It is the secret to speeding up your evolution, and it is the key to ascension. Give thanks for all that delights you and all that annoys you and terrifies you as well, and you will ascend out of all the illusion that separates you from receiving your Divine Destiny, your birthright as a Child of God.

To bring in the vibration of Gratitude, close your eyes and imagine you are looking at the most magnificent rainbow you have ever seen. Become one with the rainbow. Hug the colors, merge with them, and play with them. Spread the rainbow colors out like a great blanket, pile up all the problems you are trying to be grateful for, wrap them up, and send them as a gift to Heaven. Watch the multicolored package soar higher and higher until it disappears. As

soon as the first rainbow leaves, a new one will appear. Imagine that you once again merge with the colors, slide down the rainbow, and land in a great sea of golden Light.

Greet all the Angels waiting for you, and imagine the scenes of the life you desire to live on Earth bubbling up to meet you out of the golden sea. Smile and breathe and say inside, "I Am giving thanks for MY Highest Joy and Good." Fly High!

MESSAGE 11

FORGIVENESS

Forgiveness is about opening your mind to the experience and embodying the other person's perception of what is happening. Angels know that everyone is standing in their correct place, seeing through the filter of their own life. The valley looks deep and far away from the mountain precipice, and the precipice looks high and formidable from down inside the valley. We are here to help you to see and feel from all sides and depths, both from the selfish and selfless, from the righteous and the worthless.

We ask you to practice the experience called Forgiveness by remembering to treasure your own precious Self. Mother Father God loves you from a place of inexhaustible comfort and compassion. God wants to change how critical, judging, and inflexible humans are with themselves, and so God offers Divine Love in the vibration of Forgiveness to calm you and show you another way. When you are held in the hands of God, in the hands of Love, We see you begin to feel secure, and gradually you begin to let go of comparing yourself to others.

As you allow Forgiveness to enter, you will transform feelings of being cheated, beaten up and neglected by another, or by your Self, or by Mother Father God.

To live with an unburdened heart, humans must first forgive themselves for abusing their own sacred temple, i.e. the physical, mental, emotional, and spiritual vessel you call you. As you are made from God and in the image of God, how can you be any less than God?

Second, humans need to forgive God for sending them to Earth to experience duality, fear, and separation from Heaven. You are here as brave healers and warriors to transform Earth back to its original destiny, and We do know how very difficult your work is. Mother Father God asks your forgiveness and for your courage to complete the re-creation of the Garden of Heaven. When you remember who you are and what your mission here is all about, you can never hurt another for you have stopped hurting yourself.

Welcome to Forgiveness, carry it within you always, and wear it on your sleeve wherever you may go.

Imagine you are looking at yourself naked in a long mirror. Invite the Violet Fire of Forgiveness to pour from the top of your head (from your own crown chakra) and pour down into the image of yourself reflected in the mirror. See yourself turn completely purple and say to your vulnerable, Naked Self, "I Forgive You." Feel the new Self in the mirror walk through the looking glass and merge with your heart. Invite all who need your forgiveness to meet you in the mirror. Wash away your hurt as you wash away their blindness, deafness, and unfeelingness. Say again and again, "I forgive you." Violet is the color of Forgiveness, and YOU are the essence of LOVE! Blessings fair beauty, sweet precious Child of God.

MESSAGE 12

ONE GOD

Human beings seem to enjoy pointing out ways where they are different from one another. Some believe their way of living life is the correct way for everyone. Some desire that everyone know God through their beliefs and values, and some understand that finding God is a most personal experience.

We of the Angelic Kingdoms are truly optimistic you will be brave enough to walk your own path home to God. One God, one Mother Father, has infinite capability to love you and only you, while completely loving all the other millions of inhabitants of Family Earth at the same time.

We encourage you to look for God's face in the rainbow of color found in the faces of Earth's children, the diverse panorama of yellow, white, brown, black, and red. Listen to their rich voices, all telling many different stories of how God lives. You are brother or sister to every human being living on Earth; when you stumble across someone homeless, in mind, body, or spirit, remember that everyone is homeless until all human beings are safely nestled back home with God.

And when you see another face of God struggling with pain or poverty of any kind, reach down to the God force in your soul and shower that face with loving kindness. Pay attention to where you are walking and to what Mother Father is teaching you on your journey home to God. It requires tremendous courage to acknowledge that Divine Love is taught through many vehicles, through many teachers, and We ask you to voice your name for God in your own language.

Whether you arrive home to your Center in the name of Jesus or in the name of Buddha, crying or laughing, running or in a wheelchair, your Mother Father will greet you with open arms and a full banquet for your celebration. Find your path, follow your Truth, and know that one God loves you always, with infinite grace.

Close your eyes, and see your face as bright and smiling. You have a full set of beautiful teeth with an extra shiny gold tooth right in the front. Imagine that your smiling face is telling everyone you meet, "I Am one with God and so are you." Close your eyes and send your happy expression to all the countries of the world.

Keep smiling, and show those teeth!

MESSAGE 13

IN GOD'S TIME

When you pray for yourself or a loved one to break free from limiting patterns of thought or action, We give you Our promise your prayer will manifest at the time and in the way that is for the highest joy and good of all concerned.

Each individual soul carries perfectly orchestrated time points of exactly when the human personality will open and maintain a conscious awareness of its God potential. Awakening is a process of initiation and activation, atom by atom, cell by cell. Your process, the ignition and blazing of your Fire, is intricately woven with the process and progress of all. If you could see humanity from Our perspective, you would see a pulsing Light made of tiny sparkling sparks of Fire of all colors. Divine timing is understanding and accepting the synchronicity of the universe, all the fiery sparks ignited right on schedule. You create a brighter spark every time you allow God, expressed by your own soul, to be in charge.

Manifestation of your prayers is dependent upon the awakening of the whole human family and by your individual desire to know and love your Self more completely. Angels and Mother Father God hear your each and every prayer, and We ask you to find your Divine Will and know all requests are answered in God's time. Remember that because Mother Father God sees the big picture of your life, often you may experience something better than you prayed for.

Imagine someone you love, someone you are concerned about, sleeping soundly on a cozy violet bed. The thick Violet Fire blankets are pulled up over the loved one's head, and you can even hear the person snoring. Call on the Angel Gabriel, and she will appear with huge gold cymbals. She will hand you a set of beautiful crystal bells, and together you will give the wake-up call. Hear the cymbals crash together as you ring the crystal bells three times. Each

time Gabe hits the cymbals together, sparks of all different colors will flow into the covers and into the body and mind of the sleeping loved one. See the loved one's body rise up in the Light and proclaim with that person, "I Am awake!"

MESSAGE 14

Free Will

The will of the Ego is called free will. Free will gives the illusion that the Ego is completely free to do whatever the mind chooses.

Free will can be transformed into God's Will, the will of your heart at any moment. In truth, God's Will has authority over free will because Mother Father God knows that misdirected free will only keeps you running in circles. If you decide to jump off a cliff during a moment of despair and if it is God's Will for your soul to stay on Earth, someone will intervene in your free-will choice to die.

Willpower is about choice, instinctively choosing what is for your greatest good and focusing your intention to manifest what you desire. We believe you can direct your will to accomplish anything. Trading in free will for the Will of God allows you to conquer all obstacles on your path to freedom of body, mind, heart, and spirit. God's Will sets you free to create the life your heart united with your mind chooses to live. When the choices you make come from your Center instead of from a place of fear, you will attract wonderful opportunities to experience life's greatest treasures.

To allow God's Will to be your free will, imagine you are sitting on an exquisite violet throne. You have many rings of gold and silver on your fingers. You are looking through a doorway at your grand kingdom. You are satisfied and filled with peace and harmony because you are using your God power for the highest joy of all. Breathe in your wealth and say inside, "My will is God's Will!"

We believe in you and know you are willing to receive your freedom!

MESSAGE 15

Facing Your Shadow Self

Fear's aspects of negative thinking, low self-worth, and envy are often given credit for destroying what is good and joyous. We are here to teach you, fear is your greatest teacher. The human soul is born without fear, although it retains memory of what separation looks like and feels like. When the human soul arrives on Earth, it is wrapped in a blanket of Mother God's Light and Music. This blanket of Love is so tender and compassionate, it can attract a blanket of fear to love and to heal. The older the soul, meaning the more lifetimes spent on Earth, the more courage the soul holds within. We ask old souls to attract thick and dense layers of fear and transform these layers back into love.

The Shadow Self is the blanket of fear's negative energy your soul agreed to learn from and eventually transform. It is this condensed layer of fear that separates the Ego from Mother Father God. Your Shadow is willing to be dissolved by love as soon as you recognize fear as illusion. Ask to meet your Shadow and become its friend. Shadow has many secrets, for really your Shadow knows exactly where you are stuck in your inhibitions and insecurities. When you feel brave enough to change and break through your attachments and all the fears you resist, your Shadow will reveal all you need to see about what imprisons your Ego Self. When the Ego knows with thought, emotion, and action it is one with God, your soul is FREE!

Why does Shadow want to tell you what you are in the dark about? Shadow is really God's Energy feeling disconnected and lost, and Shadow wants to come home to the Light and Sound of Divine Love. When you become aware of how Shadow tricks you, then you are ready to face fear and clean all the sticky gum of Self-sabotage off the bottom of your shoes. When your shoes are clean, your Soul is ready to race ahead and bring you your greatest Destiny. Shadow has the key. Shadow knows all.

Imagine you are sitting in the dark. Take a deep breath, and welcome your Shadow Self to come forth from every place inside your mental body. Ask the question, "Shadow, what gift, what insight do you have for me? Why did I sabotage myself here in this situation?" After you are finished talking to your shadow, it is time for Shadow-shrinking. Visualize a Violet Fire grenade with a bright gold Light pin. Say, "Thank you, Shadow!" Pull the pin, and watch Shadow explode in Mother Father God's Violet Fire of Transformation and Forgiveness.

Message 15 is included on the audio CD.

MESSAGE 16

TRUST

Do you remember the day Gabriel delivered your soul to Earth? You were asked to leave the Angels' heavenly cocoon of unconditional love to be a brave warrior for Peace on Earth. Your soul emerged on Earth to discover a brand new environment where love is given when the conditions suit the giver. When you took form as a vulnerable baby, you naturally looked to your human mother and father for the same quality and infinite quantity of Love you experienced in Heaven.

Soon you discovered that your Earth parents were not capable of heavenly loving because they had forgotten what the love of Mother Father God feels like. Losing trust in God begins with losing trust in your human family because they are not emotionally and physically available to you at all times. When you were unable to change your outer world to match the Heaven you just left, you started to question if God is real.

Now is the moment to experience that Mother Father God's Love exists here on Earth just as it does in Heaven. Call on your Guardian Angels at all times and in all situations. Ask Us to present you with tangible evidence; miracles *can* happen in your mundane world. As you see your prayer requests answered, trust in God returns. Angels are like the hands and arms of Mother Father God, and each time you invite Us into your Self, We flood your whole vessel with unconditional love.

As you experience miracles in your daily life, We believe it is likely you will call on Us more often. We are hopeful prayer will become as automatic as breathing and before humanity knows it, God's Love will feel secure and dependable.

Close your eyes, and focus your attention on feeling your heartbeat. Imagine you are suspended in a enormous ball of peach Light of Serenity and Satisfaction. Continue to focus on listening to your

heart, and roll around in the peach Light as you feel the ball sail gently through space. Enjoy your journey. Please do travel unencumbered, and open your heart to the miracle of Trust.

Walking on Water

Which would you choose, a gravel path or a flowing river to walk on? You would probably choose the gravel path because it appears solid and familiar. You are in control of where you are going because you have walked on the path before. Humans are trained to take control and stay in control by keeping their surroundings feeling safe and familiar. Life will feel secure only if plans are made for the future and the future looks like the past.

We of the Angelic Kingdoms do not understand why humans wish to carry their past with them into their future. From Our perspective, We hope you will always be open to receiving more joy and more love. Why not enjoy something new and delightful and fulfilling each moment of your day? Angels will always choose to set down the souls of Our feet in the flowing river of living in the moment.

Would you like to walk with Us on the Holy Waters of Faith? You will soon discover no control, anxiety, or manipulation is needed. Effortlessly, you will move with the flow and have no need to see where you are going. Faith is trusting that you are exactly where you need to be, experiencing all that is for your greatest good and expansion as a Child of God.

Walking on the Water of Faith is scary at first because you feel so light when the gravity of your past is gone. Come and experience. We will never let go of your hands. We will totally support you, and gradually as the controlling thoughts of your Ego mind dissolve in Faith, you simply won't imagine traveling through life any other way.

Imagine packing boxes with all your old concepts of how life is supposed to be lived. Pack your boxes with your family secrets and co-dependent trappings. Pack up your thoughts of separation and inferiority and superiority. Pack up your addictions and attachments, and pack up all your worries about your future. Pack them all up and tie them with a golden chord of Light. Merlin arrives

with his Violet Fire (God's Light of Transformation and Forgiveness) pickup truck and helps you carry all your boxes to the river of Faith. He helps you throw the boxes into the fast-moving golden Light stream.

Watch them dissolve and when the last one is in, call on your Angels and dance upon the Holy Waters of Faith. Say inside, "I Am the miracle of Faith!"

MESSAGE 18

Manifestation

Earth is like an enormous stage where you can act out all the experiences you need to expand your human consciousness. Your OverSoul is writing the screenplay of your outer reality every moment. All your experiences are designed with perfect accuracy and synchronicity to allow you to see and feel where you are giving away your God power. Your outer reality works like a mirror by reflecting back to you where you still believe you are separate from God. As you expand your whole Self, humanity expands and each human soul gradually reunites with its OverSoul, bringing Earth and Heaven together in the consciousness of the human mind.

Manifestation is using God's Energy to bring your hopes and ideals into physical form. The more connected you become to your

OverSoul, the easier it is for you to manifest your ideals consciously and instantly. This means having the ability to create with your heart and mind your outer experiences before they happen. Masters have lived and are present in your world who can visualize what they desire, focus their God force, and have their desire appear in their hands. Angels believe all humans have this ability, and yet We ask you to not let magic distract you. Use the magic of God's Love to create a new world by trusting that all you desire to manifest will come in a way that is for the greatest good and highest joy for all.

Manifestation demands responsibility to the voice of God within you. Learn to be quiet and hear this voice, and you will be much wiser about what you ask to experience here on Earth.

Imagine you and the child within your heart standing together under a bright white Light. The white Light is so brilliant, it is all you can see. Hold both sets of your hands up to the Light. Feel the Love come inside you until you become one with each other and one with the Light of Divine Love. In your hands, hold up to the Light what you desire, and say once, "I Am giving thanks this gift manifests for me in God's time for the greatest good of all."

MESSAGE 19

Money

Money was created by the human race as a symbol for the exchange of service. The energy of performing the service or making the material product is given a value based on the supply and demand of the service or product. We ask you to consider your worth as a Child of God. What value is your creative God force worth to you?

Angels believe your value is so great, We find it impossible to place a price tag on you. As Heaven and Earth come together again on your planet, We know you will begin to value your creative gifts as God values you. How you decide to express your God force on your planet affects the vibration or quality of energy you are exchanging with your world. Fear's hindrances of jealousy, laziness, greed, doubt, and unworthiness can affect the quality of your service, your talent, and the energy you are exchanging with another.

For example, if weapons, drugs, or slavery are being traded for money, the money received will have a value equal to death and imprisonment. If human creativity in the vibration of love, empowerment, and grace is being traded, the money received will multiply for the giver and receiver.

From Our perspective, human beings give money an enormous sense of power and respect. To increase your worldly wealth, face your fears of lack of money and allow yourself to experience the generousity of the universe. The stronger your fear of not having enough money, the more resistance you have to receiving it and keeping the supply and demand of your money in balance.

When you fully remember you are made of Mother Father God's Divine Love, your wealth comes with a continuous flow. You will always have enough and more of all this physical world and the spiritual world have to offer. In order to fully remember your supreme worth, you are asked to let go of what your Ego Self is most afraid of losing. Money comes when you obey the creative calling of your soul. It is a true and wise saying, "When you follow your heart, money follows." Open and Receive.

Imagine gathering up all your debts and placing them in a boiling vat of Violet Fire soup. As you stir the soup, surrender your fears of where the money to pay the bills will come from. Remember Violet Fire is Mother Father God's Light of Transformation. When the soup is done, the color will change to bright gold Light. Drink a cup of gold Light soup and say inside, "I Am worthy to receive God's Energy in abundance today."

MESSAGE 20

ENERGY IN BALANCE

The human Self has both male and female energy. Female energy is intuitive and receptive, and male energy is active and giving. Divine Law requires that when you give of your life force, the quality of energy you give must be balanced with the quality of energy you receive.

For example, if a woman serves her partner and her family and does not nurture herself or receive equal service from her partner and family, she will lose her health, her money, her freedom, or her beauty. We ask you to consider Mother Earth as just such a woman. It is essential to continuously balance the male and female energy inside the human vessel to assist in restoring harmonious energy for Mother Earth.

Your planet needs to receive your love and nurturing to balance all the natural resources she is constantly giving. The spirit of Mother Earth is an Angel, and all Angels are Mother Father God's servants. We are constantly giving love to you, and We are constantly receiving love from God, for We are one. Invite Us to help you balance your male and female energy, giving and receiving, serving and replenishing, so your sweet planet Earth can continue to share her rich harvest with you.

Imagine your Self as an enormous Angelic Being. You are floating on your back in an ocean of ruby red Holy Spirit. Soak up Mother God's power and healing Energy into your back, the female area of your vessel. When you feel completely saturated, imagine your Self standing up, straight and mighty, and holding Mother Earth in your hands. Send her white gold Light of Divine Love out through the front of your body, the male area of your vessel. Say inside, "I Am one with God, and I give thanks my energy is in balance for the greatest good of all."

MESSAGE 21

Euphoria

Heaven is a majestic and beautiful place for little children to play. We invite you to come and be with Us here in Our Home of Joy. Inside the human heart chakra is a magical space, a doorway that gives you access to Heaven and to grand palaces existing all over the Cosmos. Heaven vibrates at a most lovely sound, a perfect set of tones always in tune with Divine Love and Peace. Heaven is a dimension where love and peace and Oneness with all of God's Creation allow only feelings of joy and satisfaction to be.

Being is about Heaven, and Being is about allowing your Self to believe for a moment that Heaven is a real place. Visiting here takes a little practice because you must come as a little child. You must allow your Self to be vulnerable and willing to leave behind worry and pain.

humans cry when they first visit Our home, and sometimes they feel physical pains in their hearts and dizzy in their brains. These sensations happen because the Love is so great, We have to open you up so you can let Our love in. The more you come and play with Us, the higher you fly.

Angels find visiting Heaven works much better than drugs and alcohol for easing mental stress and emotional and physical pain. The effects last much longer, and you will discover that you return feeling incredibly rested and inspired about your earthly work and life.

Come and experience Angel magic, and allow Us to show you that Heaven is a real place where you are always welcome. Yes, it is true you can visit loved ones living here with Us at any time during your visit. You will learn that your loved one knows exactly what has been happening for you on Earth. We have no boundaries here. Come, We will show you how to find Heaven's door inside of you. You will feel like a new person.

Close your eyes, and take in three deep breaths. As you breathe, imagine a huge wooden door opens on your heart and you walk inside. You enter a cozy emerald green room, and a little child waits

for you. Find the child, and together look for the door in the ceiling of the bright green room. The door opens, and a gold Light streams down. Stand together in the Light, and you will be lifted up and out through the door in the ceiling. When you arrive in Heaven, say inside the words, "I Am Euphoria, I Am one with Mother Father God." We are so looking forward to playing with you!

MESSAGE 22

Living in the Promised Land

Have you ever noticed how much time you spend living inside your mind? Human beings are constantly analyzing thoughts and feelings, processing their process, and exploring via the mental Self their relationship to nature, God, and humanity. God designed the human brain to function as an organic computer with the capacity to connect with Creation anywhere in the Cosmos.

Your mysterious computer has gradually shut down much of this ability in order to facilitate all your thoughts of judging yourself and comparing yourself to others. The greatest machine on Earth is preoccupied with evaluating where you are not good enough to call yourself a Child of God. Days turn into weeks and months of resisting your Divine Destiny because your brain is so busy with frustrated thinking because you do not have what you want. When your mind is clear, and judging, comparing, and wanting are escorted out the exit door, you will find yourself enjoying the promised land of a free mental body.

We ask you to imagine what your daily life would be like if you were to stop judging your Self. When you open your mind and ask for spiritual guidance, Angels will tell you that judgment is unkind and unnecessary for your walk home to finding God. Comparing your Self to others creates competition and tells you to be like everyone else.

Angels do not understand this need for comparison because We know that you are not created to be like any other person in your world. You are the best one for the task at hand, and this task is for your greatest good or you would be doing something else. Wanting serves to tell you what you wish to create, but if you allow your wanting to control your mental Self, happiness can only visit for brief moments. You always will be wanting more to feel happy. We wish to teach you how to free your mental Self so that you can connect effortlessly with all people, animals, plants, rocks, and things.

We will show you how to live in the promised land of peaceful, joyful mental satisfaction.

Breathe out like you are blowing up a balloon, and breathe in as deep as you can. Imagine your entire head is exploding in Violet Fire, God's Light of Transformation. Breathe out again, and breathe in deeply like it is your last breath before diving underwater. Again, imagine your entire head exploding in Violet Fire and say inside, "I Am all I Am, I Am all I need, I Am all I want, I Am one with God."

Repeat the entire process as many times a day as you like. You will quickly discover how positive your thoughts about life become (and it is likely your sinuses will clear for you too).

MESSAGE 23

Death

Death of the human spirit begins at birth. Spirit is the human will to live freely, and it is your spirit that resurrects you from death. It is spirit that calls and says, "Be brave and face all the murderers running rampant inside of you." How often do you attack your Self during one hour? How many times have you attracted death by seeing only the negative, only the dark, and only the fear?

Death brings transformation from one way of understanding to a higher, deeper, and broader view of life. The human soul is immortal, and as it journeys through life, it brings birth where there has been death, and it brings clarity where there has been confusion.

Expansion is a gift of transformation, and so We ask you to welcome change for the greatest good in your lives. We ask you to stop resisting the death of the attackers of your Self's esteem. All of your old concepts of belief in limitations and unworthiness and hierarchical structures are ready to die. Death is one of God's most loving miracles, for it ends suffering on all levels. We see it is not physical death that concerns humanity, it is the resistance to letting go of the fear that causes pain.

We are here to remind you of your immortality, and We ask you to cherish the physical, emotional, mental, and spiritual temple of God you are living in. How can you help your temple feel one with God with every breath, thought, and feeling? Resurrect your spirit and your life by stopping all the ways you destroy God's Creation of the human being. With the death of every fear, comes love and bliss and life eternal.

Imagine you are standing in a field in the southwest of the United States. Ahead of you stands a great platform, a funeral pyre for your death. Next to the platform is a medicine bowl, a bowl as big as the Grand Canyon. Dancing and singing around the funeral

pyre are your Guardian Angels and the Archangel Ezekiel, the Angel of Death and Transformation. Your Angels call you to walk up the steps of the platform and throw into the bowl all the memories, illusions, limiting beliefs, and parts of your Self you wish to transform.

Climb the steps, and lie down on the platform on the soft blanket of many colors. Close your eyes and say inside, "I Am releasing." Imagine that you totally dissolve in the Angel Fires in a rainbow of color. When the process is complete, you will see your Self standing in white Light in the middle of a beautiful garden. The medicine bowl has been transformed into a beautiful golden cup. Inside the Holy Grail is the ruby red Light, the Holy Spirit, Divine Essence of Mother God. Drink in the Light into your whole Self, body, mind, heart, and spirit. Say inside the words, "I Am Love." You are now a brand new Temple of God.

MESSAGE 24

BEAUTY

We will now tell you a story. Once upon a time, long ago, a beautiful child was born. This child was happy and loved to sing and draw colorful pictures of himself. He would give himself all different colors of hair in the drawings. He would draw himself short, tall, round, and square. He was a child of variety, and sometimes he would even draw himself as a she. He enjoyed showing his pictures to everyone he met, and each person always asked, "Who is this person?" The little child smiled and replied, "It is me, they are all pictures of me!"

Angels love human beings because your personalities are so fantastic and can change as fast as the weather! With personality and talent, you are constantly creating new inventions, styles, menus, and ways of thinking about what you have created. Beauty is humanness, and as We look at you and love you, We see such loveliness and grace. We are optimistic We can convince you to look at your Ego Self as a gift from God, special and perfectly designed to illustrate Divine Love through your personality.

When you gently reassure your Ego that your personality is attractive and worthy, your Ego smiles like the little child in the story. The Ego says, "It is me, they are all pictures of Me." As you love your "Me," you become integrated with your "I Am," and together you are united with God and united with your world. Allow your Self to acknowledge your beauty and your talents. Give your Self the gift of knowing that no one else can compare with you, for truly you are the most beautiful in all your land.

Breathe in deeply, and exhale slowly. Imagine you are on stage standing in a brilliant spotlight of the color you look best in. The audience is filled with faces of your Self and everyone is cheering for you. The applause is deafening, and as the flowers land at your feet, smile and breathe and say inside, "I Am so very beautiful!"

MESSAGE 25

CURING ADDICTION

Addiction originates from longing to be one with God. Only Divine Love can fill your heart, soul, and mind with completeness and joy. Humans have tried every thing imaginable to fill the void created by separation from God. You have tried using drugs, work, sex, relationship, sacrifice, entertainment, money — and the list continues — of false substitutes for Divine Love. These "medicines" do not last, and so you try more of what does not work. If someone you love chooses to drink to quiet feelings inside, look inside your own Self for your own avoidance strategies. How do you escape from the nagging voice telling you about your misery, your own incompleteness?

The cure for addiction is to first find the courage to admit you are addicted to fear. Without your fears, you would be free to go and do exactly what your heart desires.

The Angelic detox center is always open. When you enter Our home, We will fill you up with love and gently show you that you are not alone. As you remember your Oneness with Mother Father God, you automatically let go of chemical, material, and relationship crutches you have desperately needed. The root of your addiction comes from believing you were abandoned by Divine Love, and no earthly substance can substitute for the real thing. Curing addiction is simple because there is only one cure: Oneness with your God Self.

Be brave enough to ask for Our help, and We will begin Our treatment of God's healing Love. We are looking forward to celebrating your recovery and the recovery of all people on your planet, present, past, and future. Heaven on Earth is Our promise, and Angels always keep Their promises!

Imagine you are a tree and your legs and feet are your roots. Ask Archangel Michael to come and cut down the tree that is you. He takes the roots and soaks them in boiling Violet Fire, God's Light

of Transformation and Forgiveness. With the upper part of the tree that is you, he places the trunk and branches in warm ruby red Light, the Fire of Love and Compassion from Mother God. As you feel your tree parts soaking in the colors, say inside these words, "I Am one with God with my whole Tree of Life." Michael will put you back together and then see your Self as a strong, healthy Tree of gold and green Light.

Send your roots deep down into Mother Earth, raise your branches up high into the warmth of Father Sun, and say, "I Am one with God."

MESSAGE 26

God's Child

From the beginning, your heart has remained in the heart of your Mother Father God. As you grew from two cells into a fetus into an infant and on to an adult, loving embraces flowed from God's Center into your Center. Inside your heart lives a little child filled with Divine Love, and she is waiting to share all this abundance with you. Any abuse, neglect, or hardship you may have suffered throughout your life covers the little child inside your heart.

We wish to show you how to lift the cover of hurt off your heart so you can feel all the love you have been missing, all the love you have been waiting for. God's Child within your heart is a voice to your subconscious, to the past you have forgotten. God's Child is the doorway to direct communication with your OverSoul, always guiding you from Heaven.

Angels specialize in helping humans find their broken hearts, mend them, and transform them into brand new. We are here to teach you how to love the child within you as God loves you, as an only child. It is not necessary for you to revisit the past; just lift the cover, and find God's Child resting peacefully in Mother Father God's generous lap of Everlasting Love. Come with Us. We have someone We wish you to meet. He wants to play with you and teach you about the miracles of Heaven. She knows all the dreams about your future, and she is the Magic One who can make them come true for you.

Close your eyes, and imagine walking into a tunnel made of beautiful stones of all shapes and colors. The tunnel leads into an emerald green ocean of Light. As you enter the green Light, look for a coral colored oyster shell and pop open the lid. Inside lives God's Child, the child of your heart. She might need you to shower her with gentle Violet Fire rain drops to wash away old pain.

When he is free, play and play and play in the green Light. Enjoy and do try and visit him each day. She has much to tell you!

MESSAGE 27

Cleaning House, Angel Psychotherapy

Human beings have a great storage capacity for holding onto old feelings because humans do not understand how to let go of pain. Painful emotions must be cleared from the mental and emotional bodies, or their energy will be soaked up by the cells in your physical body. It is instinctive for you to resist processing hurt feelings because you are trying to protect yourself from the fear of being hurt again.

Frequently the Ego Self convinces you to forget or ignore the experience, and often you continue to attract new experiences that bring up the same feelings you tried to ignore. Abandoned feelings will seep out like toxic waste until they are completely transformed into forgiveness and Love. For example, when your ideas or feelings are rejected by someone you care about, this disappointment opens the vault of cellular memory of any time in your past where you felt unappreciated. Your Shadow Self grabs onto the hurt and sends out the belief that you will continue to experience more rejection in the future.

Unresolved painful experiences and the fear they will repeat creates separation between you and your God Self.

We desire for you to experience feelings of joy and believe your life will continue to improve and open. Knowing that Mother Father God lives within you and all around you is essential for creating Heaven's miracles in your life. We of the Angelic Kingdoms offer you Our housecleaning service. We are efficient, courteous, and reliable and know where all the cobwebs are hiding.

ANGELIC HOUSE CLEARING: (music is required) *Close your eyes, and breathe in deeply and slowly. Imagine you are stepping into a bubbling Violet Fire pool of God's Light. As you soak in the Violet Fire, imagine your whole vessel — mental, emotional, and physical — is a giant sponge saturated with old emotion. Ask your Guardian Angel to come and wring out the sponge. When the*

sponge is empty, soak up more Violet Fire into your every pore and again ask your Angel to wring out the sponge. Continue as long as you like, and you may find it helpful to focus on certain feelings or experiences.

MESSAGE 28

Loving your pets

Pets are Nature Angels devoting their lives to assisting humans in the healing of their emotional Selves. Animals and plants and even inanimate pets soak up stress and fear for you, and they are constantly relaying messages from Angels and Mother Father God. Animals, both domestic and wild, work diligently to help clear and transform the negative energy generated from fearful thought into love and kindness.

City rats have a great deal of responsibility, and so We are hopeful you will send them a bit of gratitude. They symbolize clearing emotional garbage generated by wasteful thought, and so they eat out of trash cans and live in sewers. The family dog and cat hold a much more respectable status because they live in a sheltered environment.

Your family pets are sensitive to your thoughts and feelings, and they will mirror back to you what you might not see. For example, cats are a metaphor for feelings, as they are felines. If your cat enjoys sitting in the middle of your work papers, perhaps you need to give your feelings a little attention. When you are looking for some Divine Guidance from an earthly perspective, talk to your family pet, the wildlife around your neighborhood, or the animals at the zoo. Talking to animals and plants requires concentration on really listening.

Your pets understand every word you speak to them, and they can hear every thought you think. They may not always choose to listen, just as you may not always choose to listen to them or to your inner Self. We are delighted to have the opportunity to teach you how to communicate with the world of Nature Angels living with you and all around you.

Sit comfortably with your pet and ask if now is a good time for a chat. The pet will give you a signal of yes or no. Send love energy straight from your heart, and feel the vibration of love that comes back. Ask your pet either out loud, or with your thoughts, a question. The answer will come through in your own

thought because animals communicate telepathically and most often using mental images.

Give thanks for God's Creation, and God's Creation will show thanks to you!

MESSAGE 29

Angels' Keys to Success

Angels are successful with Our work of performing miracles because We truly believe in what We are doing. We know without a doubt that We are working for the highest joy and good of all. We love Our work, for it brings Us great joy, and so We have nothing to complain about.

Our first key to your success is to listen to your heart at all times and follow your Truth.

Our second key is to stop complaining and making excuses for why you cannot follow your heart.

Our third key is to allow yourself to receive for what you give and to ask for this exchange to be in balance.

Our fourth key is to remember that all money comes from Mother Father God and that God is the source of your paycheck.

Our fifth key is to allow your Self to express your creative talents and share God's gifts with the world. Everyone does want what you have to share, so if you enjoy your craft, continue. If you are miserable at what you do, ask your Self why you are forcing yourself to do work that compromises your integrity.

Our sixth key is to know what you are responsible for and allow others to do their own work, even if you feel you can do a better job.

Our last key, number 7, is to ask for Angelic assistance throughout your day. For every creative concept, a Deva Angel is ready to help you manifest it here on Earth. Angels love to smooth out the rough edges, cut through red tape, and bring Truth and justice to Light for all to see.

Serve from your heart and ask to know how your daily work contributes to humanity. When you have a sense of Divine Purpose, your success is certain and heavenly!

Either mentally or on a piece of paper, record all the reasons why you cannot be successful doing what your heart desires. Please

include any old family beliefs or fears and fears concerning financial support. Imagine you burn the list in God's Violet Fire of Transformation and Forgiveness and say inside, "I Am free to Be who I Am." Now imagine you are totally immersed in a bright turquoise Light. Turquoise is the Angel Fire of Success and this energy helps to release your God Willpower, courage, and your worthiness. Say inside, "I Am Fame and Fortune for the greatest good of all concerned!"

MESSAGE 30

REFUELING

Humans have been taught for ages to sacrifice their needs for the needs, wants, and demands of others. With sacrifice comes denial of Self, feelings, and connection to God. When the human Self is neglected, exhaustion and eventual illness can overtake the emotional and physical bodies.

To refuel your vessel, Angels recommend you begin by allowing yourself to feel. Feelings can show you where you are believing you are less powerful or less worthy than another. All feelings are sacred because your emotional Self is directly connected to the spiritual body. Connecting to spirit solely via the mind no longer works. The Divine Feminine Force is returning to your planet, meaning Mother

God's Energy of Emotion is balancing with Father God's Energy of Thought on Earth.

In ages past, students of spiritual enlightenment could expand their intuitive ability just by thinking. Now, in the Age of Heaven on Earth, all students expand by feeling their feelings and balancing emotion with intellect. Intimate Oneness with Mother Father God happens when you put God first in your daily life; this means nurturing your whole vessel and taking time to listen to the voice of God within you.

We remind you that sacrifice and denial of feeling are natural responses for you. We are in your life to assist you in healing every aspect of your Self. Call on Us, and We will show you how to allow God, your own Center, to guide you and nourish you. It is only when you are full that you can give to others. If you are empty, you have nothing to offer. We welcome you to experience Angelic refueling. It is like visiting a healing spa inside yourself anytime you like.

ANGEL SPA

Imagine you are lying on a bed of the thickest, softest green moss you have ever seen. Begin to breathe in deeply and exhale slowly. The Cherubim Angels will come and gently hook you up to the

"Holy Spirit I.V." intra-vessel recharge with Mother God's unconditional Love. Allow the green Light of Healing and the Holy Spirit to completely saturate you inside and out. Say inside, "I Am soaking up Love, Love and more Love." Invite your feelings to come forth from deep inside you, listen, and release.

MESSAGE 31

PARENTING

The individual human being deserves freedom to Be. Parenting is about creating a sacred space for a child to grow and discover his or her God potential. Every person wants to be taken care of, to be listened to, and loved for who one is, not just for what one gives you. We ask you to remember with a compassionate heart, true desire is calling, "Please, take care of me." Whether you are the most independent and courageous or whether you cannot leave your house without all-weather gear and a companion at your side, you want with all your heart for loving parents to take care of you and protect you.

Angels are parents who are available at all times and in all situations, for We never have headaches, and We never throw Our backs out. Children of all ages need Our loving parenting, and so We offer Our complete devotion to you and to your family.

When you are exhausted and need comforting and a baby-sitter is nowhere to be found, call on Us. We will come and watch your child and help you to release the stress, worry, and burden of feeling overwhelmed by life. Human parents become healthier and wiser teachers when they allow their Angels and Guides to mother and father them. We will joyously prove to you, you are not alone. All children are Mother Father God's Children, and God's Love can provide all the support you need and want both spiritually and physically.

Be wise and loving parents, and give your children space to grow. Encourage them to remember that because God lives inside of them, they need to treat themselves with tremendous respect, and this goes for you too. Enjoy being a child for your whole life and know We are protecting and loving you always!

HAPPY NAP-TIME

Close your eyes, and imagine you are curled up next to your Guardian Angel. You are resting on a lush velvet ruby red sofa, and the pillow is just right. Breathe in the soft red color of the velvet, and feel the fabric with your hands. Say inside, "I Am the Beloved Child of Mother Father God." As you rejuvenate, you may desire to have your children come and rest with you. The ruby sofa of Mother God's Holy Spirit will grow as large as you need it to, and you will discover there is enough room for several generations. Enjoy and relax and soak up the love and protection from your Angel Parents!

MESSAGE 32

UNDERSTANDING VIOLENCE

Violence comes from repressed anger, and anger comes from feeling cheated, rejected, abandoned, and unworthy. Angels believe anger can be your greatest emotion, for you do not make changes until you are angry. When the human being is sad, guilty, depressed, embarrassed, or lonely, the situation is often tolerated until anger comes. Anger makes a human change inside and out. When anger is expressed in violence, serious harm can happen, and when the vibration of anger is raised to the vibration of volition and action, healthy change can happen for the greatest good of all concerned.

Physical violence is a reaction to feeling powerless, and so the Twelve Archangels of the Central Soul offer you a new source of power. Trade in your weapons for the Angel Power Tools, Angel energy which is all-powerful and all-loving at the same time. We suggest when you have had all you can take, when you feel you have been a victim to another's actions for too long, ask Us to help you set new boundaries for yourself. Ask yourself if the situation feels at all familiar to anything you may have experienced as a child. If the answer is yes, travel with Us back to your past, and firebomb the whole scene in your mind using Angel love bombs made of God's Violet Fire of Transformation and Forgiveness.

As you let the purple Light flood the memory, the past is transformed into love and freedom for your present. If the situation is one you are struggling with now, again throw Violet Fire bombs and blow up all people you have allowed to violate your sacred space. A bomb is a metaphor for instant transformation. When you use Violet Fire to clear another person, the Fire automatically clears your vessel of negative energy too. Angel Fire is Love, and Love heals all hurts. You will see immediate changes in your outer world, and you will feel free from past traumas you continue to carry with you.

Freedom is yours. Don't just react to violence of body, mind, heart, and spirit. Do something about it!

Close your eyes, and imagine in front of you is your arsenal of Violet Fire love-bombs, grenades, mud pies, and Violet Fire ear cleaners or cotton-tipped swabs. You might want to include adding Michael's sword and arrows of sapphire-blue Light, the Angel Fire of Truth and Awareness. Think of someone you are angry with, someone who has hurt you, and you have not been able to entirely release the experience. Throw love bombs, and shoot arrows of God's Truth until you feel your chest open and expand. Keep breathing, and as you fire away, say inside, "I Am releasing and forgiving." When you feel complete, ask your Self and your Angels how can you set healthy boundaries for your Self in the future. Welcome to Freedom and Welcome to Love!

MESSAGE 33

Falling in Love with Your Self

On the day We met, I fell in Love with you. I Am your Angel, and I Am your Guide and protector. When you connect with Me and give Me thanks, it is your Self you have discovered. Human beings and Angels, and loving kind people you meet on your path home, all reflect back to you the love bursting inside your heart, the love you feel for you. Heaven sings with you with each opening of your heart. As you open your Self to falling in Love with another, with God, with life, Heaven and Earth come a little closer.

We are delighted to assist you in falling in Love every moment of your day. The euphoric feelings tell Us you are beginning to understand who God is and who you are. Celebrate the sacred marriage between you and your heart, and love will continue to find you.

To create a fairy tale come true, first fall in love with *you*; then your prince, princess, king, or queen must come, for it is Divine Law. Oneness is a precious discovery and when you open your heart to another, Oneness happens. Be brave, and ask Us to help you create Oneness with your own mind, heart, body, and soul, and then true bliss is yours when you meet your Divine companion.

Never settle for less than what you deserve, true love, truest love. Look for your beauty reflected in the eyes of all you admire and know I Am your Angel, and together We are celebrating forever.

Close your eyes, and imagine that out from your heart flows a luscious emerald green Light of Love. Allow the Love to flow until you are one with the green Light. From above your head, the bright golden white Light of Divine Love begins to flow and swirl with the Love Light of your heart. Say inside the words, "I Am Oneness, Oneness, One." Enjoy, and remember true love is worth waiting for.

MESSAGE 34

MOM AND DAD

Inside your Center lives God. God is both Mother (Divine Emotion) and Father (Divine Thought). When you are completely connected to your Divine Mother and Father, you can fully express the power and love of God in your daily life on Earth. We of the Angelic kingdoms believe that now is the time for humanity to think and feel from the Center. To raise the vibration of your thoughts to their highest purity, pay attention to what you are thinking.

When negative or fearful thoughts come crusading into your conscious awareness, blast them with Violet Fire and transform them into Love. To open to Divine Emotion, We ask you to have the willing intention to feel your feelings without judgment or negative reaction. The power of emotion, together with pure thought, keep you in your Center, the place of trust, faith, and Oneness with all of God.

As you learn to live from your heart, you learn how to become your own loving mother and father. We will teach you how to clear out old male (thought energy) and old female (emotional energy) to make room for the Divine. Enjoy your new awareness, and remember that joy is contagious. We see you sharing your new positive attitude with all you meet. Freedom and continuous joy are yours when you think and feel from your Holy Heart space.

Imagine you transform yourself into an enormous wardrobe with doors on both the front and back. Open the door to the front, and look inside for sleeping men. They may look sick or weak or miserable. In your hands, you are holding a Violet Fire fireman's hose. Spray all the men with purple Light of Transformation and Forgiveness. Keep spraying until the wardrobe is completely clear. Now, imagine walking around to the back of the closet and opening the door. This time, you have a ruby red Fire floodlight, and when you shine the Light on any sleeping, depressed, or sick women or children, they will disappear in the Holy Spirit, the Fire of Mother

God's Love. Continue until the back of the wardrobe is completely clear, and say inside, "I welcome my Divine Mother and Father to resurrect within me." Take three deep breaths and say inside, "We are one, I Am one with Mother Father God."

Explanation of metaphor in the imagery exercise: wardrobe or closet, a symbol for what is lost or hidden in your consciousness. Sleeping men symbolize old negative and limiting thought patterns and concepts of how life is to be lived. Sleeping women and children are metaphors for repressed emotions and absorbed emotions originating from other people. Cleaning the closet with Angel Fire represents release of the old and fulfillment with Divine Love.

MESSAGE 35

Meeting Your Guardian Angels

Guardian Angels work constantly to open your heart, your mind, and your vision. The human potential amazes Us, and We are determined to bring you to your highest and most joyful potential. We are within you and all around you, reminding you that you are a Child of God. We speak to you in the occurrences and happenings of your mundane world. Everywhere you look, you can find an Angelic message of wisdom right under your nose. We teach you with your outer world, and We teach you through the faces and life experiences of all you encounter.

Angels are as real as humans are becoming, and so We call you to open, open, and open! When you call for Our assistance, miracles happen.

The human Self is not in control, and often We show you that relief comes in God's time and in God's way of manifestation. Guardian Angels help you surrender control to trusting and having faith. God keeps you safe and provides for all you need.

We recommend you do not spend your quiet time trying to see Us or hear Us speak to you in long conversations. We tell you to discover Us by opening your life to results, to long awaited changes, and action for your greatest good. When fear comes to visit, breathe and know We are present. Face your fear and let go of what you are afraid of losing. Surrender to God and listen for the answer inside of your Self. Watch as your reality changes, and once again all is well. Angels are not on Earth to bring happiness in the way your Ego expects it to appear. We are here to remind you to live in the present moment. Living in the present, without clinging to the past or constantly predicting the future, will bring you eternal joy and freedom forever and ever. Come, We will show you!

Close your eyes and breathe. Imagine a luscious gold Light gently swirling around you, lifting you up, and filling you with Love. Allow this gold Light to wash away any sticky negative thoughts or

resentments from your day. Open and say inside, "Guardian Angels, I Am ready to play." Remember We are Light and Music, and We answer in action. Try just being with Us and know We are real, as real as you are becoming!

MESSAGE 36

The Law of Attraction

Something quite miraculous happens when you allow your Self to experience life from your Center. The Center is the home of God within you, and as you live from this house, life flows with peaceful serenity. How can life on Earth possibly stay calm and joyful?

The house of God inside your heart has doors and windows impervious to fear and to attachment. Debt and pain and hurt cannot enter this home, although the solutions are often found just inside the doorway, just inside the window sill.

As Children of God, you have the power to bring to you all you need, and this is the Divine Law of Attraction. We will show you how to work with the Law, and you will need to surrender control. Control stops the magic.

When you are ready for your prayer to be answered, you will attract the experience, relationship, circumstances, career opportunity, or assistance right into your energy field, up close and personal.

When you are not ready, but your Ego believes you are, you can try to force what you want by beating the pavement, the bushes, the diner, and even the heavens, and you will still not be ready. Surrendering resistance to what you have asked for is another lesson you will learn when living in the home of God. Resistance to following your heart creates inner and outer conflict. You will continue to learn that God always wins, and control always lets go in the end. Angels are present to show you what you are resisting, for often it is wonderful and will bring you great joy. Together, breaking through resistance and attracting, effortlessly, the miracles you are ready for can make for a very satisfied human being. Home, Sweet Home.

Imagine you are ready for your daily shower and allow the water to be Michael's sapphire-blue Fire of Truth. Invite the blue Light to wash away all the truths you are resisting, all the entrapments

your Ego and Shadow Self have led you to believe about your life. Watch the resistance flow down the drain with the dirt and the soap bubbles, and say inside, "I attract from my Center all I need to come to me, effortlessly."

Message 36 is included on the audio CD.

Angel Treasury

BOOK ONE

Where Does God Come From?

PART I: INTRODUCTION

Asking where God comes from is asking your own mind, heart, body, and soul, "Where do I come from and what am I made out of?" Angels and humans and stars and oceans and black space in the night sky are all made of the same substance Angels call Energy.

God is Energy, and this Energy is the substance of all that is physical and nonphysical as well. God's Energy or Spirit or Divine Essence is exactly what God is made of and where God comes from. We will tell you much about this mystical circle, a circle without a beginning or end, a circle that breathes in and out in a most magnificent spiral of Energy.

Energy creates Light and Sound, and Light and Sound are what God is made of, and Light and Sound are where God comes from, and so do you. The Sound and Light are always together; Sound creates Emotion, and Light creates Thought.

In God are both Mother (Divine Emotion) and Father (Divine Thought), Sound, and Light. Mother God and Father God together created Divine Love, and Divine Love desired to expand God out from the realms of Spirit, Thought, and Emotion to the physical, and so Creation began. God is made of Emotion, Thought, Love, and Creation; this is where God comes from, and so do you.

Energy, Sound and Light, Emotion, Thought, Love, and Creation create the Heart of God. God's heart is filled with Divine Love, which means God has no conditions, no rules or standards for loving. Each and every particle of God's Energy is filled with Divine Love, and Love connects each particle of Energy to every other particle of Energy, which We call the experience of Oneness.

Oneness is a vibration of perfect unity, a complete connection of thought with feeling of Love and Creation. Oneness allows each particle of God's Energy to hear and feel the thoughts and feelings of every other particle of Energy. This would feel to you like you would have complete compassion and insight into every human being you meet or rock, tree, animal, or drop of water you touch.

PART II: ORIGINS

Mother and Father and Divine Love and Creation make up the whole essence of God's Energy. God sent forth the Energy, the Sound and Light in the name of Oneness and manifested many universes. Each universe is made of many particles all capable of sensing each other because Oneness connects them to the Center of God.

The Center of God's Energy is called the Central Sun or Soul, and from the Center Soul, all creation originates. God's Energy moves out as a spiral from the Center, and the spiral has an infinite number of rings of Energy, Sound, and Light. From the Central Sun, 12 Suns were created, and from these Suns or Souls of God's Energy came all the galaxies, stars, planets, and Beings of Love. It is difficult for Us to try to describe God's Creation because We see no separation. Even saying 12 Suns come from the Central Sun implies each of these Suns is separate. It is more like taking white Light and shining it through a prism to show 12 colors or rays of Light and 12 Sounds all originating from one Sound. When you then take each of these 12 Lights and Sounds and 12 twelve more from each one, you then have 144 Lights and Sounds. When mixed and played together like an orchestra filled with 144 different instruments, you can imagine how infinite God's creativity is.

Each and every particle of Energy originates from the Central Soul and has memory of the Center. Each particle is a sentient being of Light and Sound. Every moon, planet, asteroid, star is a thinking, feeling, loving, and creating Being of God. Each has its own Center, its own Soul, which connects back to the Central Soul of God.

PART III: THE TWELVE ARCHANGELS OF THE CENTRAL SUN

God manifested 12 Angelic Kingdoms from each of the 12 Souls radiating from the Center. These 12 Kingdoms of Energy produce a majestic symphony of Sound and Light and Love and they are called the Twelve Archangels of the Central Sun. Archangel means protector of Oneness; We build arches and bridges uniting all physical and nonphysical forms of creation with each other. We have awareness of all life, and We can feel and communicate with every particle of God's Energy.

It is Our responsibility to bring Earth and all her children back home to the Center of Oneness. Our work will be completed when every human thought and feeling returns to the vibration of Divine Love. Mother Father God, in unity with Divine Love and Creation, requested the assistance of the Twelve Archangels in testing the strength and resourcefulness of Oneness. This is where the story of Earth begins.

PART IV: THE STORY OF THE BEGINNING OF EARTH

One moment, Father God asked Mother God what it would be like if Thought were separate from Emotion, and Sound were separate from Light.

What would happen to Divine Love if it were separate from Creation? Would the Souls inside the stars and planets and their inhabitants forget Oneness? Would they forget where they come from?

How powerful is Divine Love and would it be strong enough to reunite all of God's particles back together?

Mother God and Father God and Divine Love and Creation decided to answer these questions by conducting an experiment called "the moment of separation from Oneness."

Deep in the heart of God, in the Central Sun, in the Center Soul, God knew this experiment was for the greatest good of all particles of Energy.

WHY?

Mother God (Divine Emotion) knew the experiment would force Divine Love to stretch Itself out from the safe Center and create new powers of the Central Soul, the powers of compassion, hope, faith, and trust.

Together, these forces of Love bring God's Energy back to Truth, the Truth that Oneness is All-loving and All-powerful. Oneness is all there is and all there ever needs to be.

PART V: THE ILLUSION OF TIME

All of God's Energy exists at one moment, as God's Energy cannot be created or destroyed. God's Energy exists in the moment, having no past or future, being all there is, and all there ever will be.

The Archangel Lucifer Michael carried forth the Will of God and created the illusion of time. Time is a thought without emotion, without love, and time is the catalyst for inventing separation. Time created the illusion of making two moments, one before and one after.

Mother Father God took a breath in these moments of before and after, and the particles of God's Energy appeared to move in a straight line with one before and one behind. The illusion gave the particles temporary amnesia so that they believed they were no longer moving in a spiral. They believed they were disconnected from the Center. During this moment of amnesia, Father God (Divine Thought) and Mother God (Divine Emotion) created the illusion of one moment of separation between them and so for one moment, Sound appeared to be separated from Light, and Thought was separated from Emotion.

A window of time lasting one breath of God was all that Lucifer Michael needed to create the sun Horus, the sun of your solar system, and from Horus, Earth and her brother and sister planets were birthed. Horus and Earth and her brother and sister planets were born in a moment where the illusion of separation from the Center of God appeared to be Reality.

After this breath, the window of time was closed, and all the particles of God's Energy, the Sound and the Light once again consciously knew they moved in a spiral, and all Souls knew they were connected to the Central Sun.

PART VI: SPLIT

Lucifer Michael designed Earth as a schoolroom where Souls could come and create a false reality, a reality fully experiencing the illusion of separation from God and from each other. Earth was to be the library for all the universes and store all learning about Creation and the great duality between Oneness and Separation.

The sun, Horus, and the other planets and moons were to protect Earth and assist her, and so the science of astrology was invented. Several other star systems as well as Earth's brothers and sisters were designed as training camps for particles of God's Energy wishing to participate in the learning process called duality.

During this instant, a mere fraction of a breath for God, the great story of illusion was established, and on the Earth, the Archangel Lucifer Michael appeared to split into two separate Angelic kingdoms.

Lucifer carried forth the Will of God and sent out the thought, "Separation from God is real," and from separation, fear was born. The experiment's design included giving human beings a brain capable of thinking fearful thoughts.

PART VII: FEAR

Neither Lucifer nor Michael nor any of the other Archangel Kingdoms knew that because fear originated from illusion, it had the fantastic ability to rapidly produce more fear. Soon, fear was casting a spell of forgetting and putting human brains to sleep. Humans began to forget Truth, the Truth that Oneness is Love and Love is all there is.

In the beginning of time on Earth, the concept of fear spread slowly because the particles of God's Energy making up the human brain remembered Oneness. As time passed, the particles started to forget they were connected to the Central Sun; they began to believe in separation, and Master Fear encouraged them to forget and create more fear.

As fear multiplied, humanity began to feel afraid of humanity, of life itself, and of God. The human mind even separated into the

Ego mind, the mind believing in fear, and the Creative mind, the mind remembering God. For many humans, the Ego mind took control. Thus, they began to forget that they are the creators of their reality, and so they were enmeshed more and more in the illusion that separation from God is real and that living life is something to be afraid of.

PART VIII: THE END OF THE EXPERIMENT

As the Creative minds of Earth's children began to go silent, so did their abilities to communicate with other particles of God existing on Earth and other planets. They began to believe in the ultimate abandonment by God and lost their awareness of their immortality. When they no longer could communicate with Oneness, the realm of Heaven disappeared and became a separate place for souls without minds and bodies, a place reachable only through death.

Some members of the human race learned how to quiet the Ego mind and become immune from fearful thoughts. Some of these same people used their remembering to take control over others, giving them the false message that they were capable of something others were not. Entire populations of people gave their minds and bodies over to rulers who threatened them with death or punishment. They gave up the power of knowing that they come from Oneness and are responsible for creating their reality on Earth.

Many Beings of Divine Love came to Earth to teach humanity the Truth again, and still fear lulled the human brain back to sleep. Each time fear's illusions caused one human being to harm another, the whole Earth would feel abandoned and alone.

Earth's feelings of desperation were instantly felt deep in the heart of God. Mother Father God, in unity with Divine Love and Creation, decided immediately to end the experiment. Because time was already part of the conscious experience of Earth, it appears one instant has lasted for millennia on your planet.

PART IX: THE LAW OF ONE

Lucifer had watched his work bring rapid destruction to the precious library of Oneness, and so he called on his other half, Michael, to establish the Law of One on Earth. This law of Mother God Father God, Divine Love and Creation allows humans to manifest only those experiences that are for the greatest good and learning of all concerned.

The knowledge of the Law of One has always lived in the Creative mind of every human being, and now is the time for you to remember this Law and bring your brain back to an understanding of Oneness. It is now time in Earth time for Heaven and Earth to be reunited and experience only what is for the highest joy and good of all.

PART X: THE SPIRAL OF SOUND AND LIGHT

When Lucifer and Michael first split, Michael was given the job of protecting the Truth. He did this by creating a door in the Creative mind that was always open, a door connecting the Creative mind to God's Energy of your soul and your soul to the Central Soul. Angels call this door your OverSoul, or Body of Sound and Light. The key to finding the door is Love, remembering to love every particle of your mental, emotional, physical, and spiritual self unconditionally.

Michael brings the Truth that each particle of energy in your brain is connected to every particle in every human brain that has lived, is living, or ever will live. As you love your Self and open the door to your Creative mind, you assist the opening of all Creative minds and of all souls. When the door is opened, the boundary between Heaven and Earth will dissolve, and humanity will be free to enjoy the great library and consciously be one with all of God.

Lucifer and Michael are now reunited on your planet and, together with all the Archangels of the Central Soul, they are here to teach you how to transform the illusion of fear and separation back to love and Oneness.

It is the Will of God for humanity to remember that God is a most magnificent spiral of Sound and Light, a symphony playing joyful music, and You are a most critical instrument in the orchestra.

The Archangels of the Central Sun invite you to experience an "Angels' Guide" to creating miracles and coming home to Heaven. We give you tools in abundance to make your journey comfortable and effortless.

Welcome!

Book One is included on the audio CD.

BOOK TWO

Heaven on Earth, Meeting the Twelve Archangels of the Central Sun

Who are We?

We call Ourselves the Twelve Archangel Kingdoms of the Central Sun or Soul of God. We are like 12 spokes connecting to a great wheel. This great wheel is suspended in a sphere of Sun Light, together making the Center Soul, the Center of Oneness, and the Center of the Cosmos.

We can stretch out Our spokes of Light and Sound and expand into an infinite number of Angels and fill all the universes in the Cosmos at the same moment. All 12 spokes of God's wheel are saturating Earth with Our Power, Light, Music, and Healing.

Coming from inside the ball of Light, from each of the twelve spokes, you can hear a beat identical in rhythm to the human heart. Our hearts sing together with yours. When We are invited into your Holy space, We fill all your auras (energy fields) with Our presence and Our heartbeat.

When Archangels embrace you, We see, feel, experience, and know everything you do. Once this connection is made, it can never be severed, and you will never be the same again.

Our energy is magical and all-penetrating; it stretches you and makes you demand to know your truth and carry it out courageously. When one of Us touches you, you will know all that God knows, and you will again see the total beauty of your planet and of your life.

Angels touch you again and again, and each time, your Light fuses with Our Light. With every sensual fusion, you are changed for the highest joy and good of all. We enjoy being your Guides and helping you to integrate the spiritual perspective of your life with the mundane.

You are Our responsibility, and We are escorting you home to the sanctuary of Divine Love found right inside your own Self.

Some of your teachers call Us Wind, Water, Mineral, Fire, and Ether. To others, Our names are Thought, Feeling, Communication, Will, Manifestation, Destruction, and Transformation. We call Ourselves "Loving

Kindness," and We are here to offer you Our healing music and energy. We look forward to walking with you and sharing God's wisdom of fully living life on Earth. You are all that We are, one power making up the mind, heart, body, and soul of Mother Father God.

We welcome you to experience Us and find the Heaven you have been waiting for. The words "I Am" mean just this. We ask you to say the words, "I Am one with God" and dance with Us here in Heaven. Come, We will talk, and you will understand. Freedom is yours when God lives inside you and you live inside God.

It is Our mission for God to prove to humanity that Heaven has always existed right inside of you. Heaven is the home of Mother Father God and all your dreams-come-true. Imagine a piece of real estate, a real estate that belongs to you. You become the caretaker and tend the land and riches and share with all you love. Together, you live in paradise, trusting in everyone you meet and living life for the greatest good of all. This Truth is Mother Father God's intention for you, and now is the time for you to face fear, the thief who stole your estate.

When you give love to this great master of illusion, the master transforms and your wealth of joyous experience expands. Fear is this master, and fear holds humanity in a spell, a spell tied and bound with just one thin chord. The chord holds you completely captive just like a puppet with only one string. Slicing through this chord is a simple feat, and then again moving mountains from one state to another would seem easier to you.

If We teach you how to cut through the chord called fear hanging around your neck, then you join in Our mission, and you will be called to go forth and teach others how to find Heaven inside themselves. In no time at all, everyone will know the secret of how to take back their estate, and Heaven will become the only home you know.

We will ask you to remember again and again, it is only one string, not many, only one fear that keeps humanity from living in complete freedom and harmony with Mother Earth. Fear is clever at trying to distract you from this simple Truth. Fear breeds complication, chaos, and confusion, and when you confront fear with its own secret, fear loses power over you.

THE SECRET

Once upon a distant plane, a place called Heaven existed both day and night. Angels and humans and stars and creatures of all colors and design walked together in peace and harmony.

During a great explosion of Sound and Light, Master Fear arrived in a blast of black smoke. He said to Heaven, "I am really an Angel in disguise, and I have come to teach you what Heaven really is". You see, "he said to all of Us, if you do not experience what it feels like to lose Oneness, then you can never truly know Heaven's grace."

The Master Fear began his work of stripping Heaven of its bounty, and We all started to sense Our foundation breaking underneath Our feet. With nothing to stand on, with nothing to rely on, We took on Our greatest fear, Our fear of abandonment. Abandonment of Mother Father God's Love and support, abandonment of Heaven from the plane of Earth, abandonment of Angels' wings of Light and protection are fear's greatest illusion.

Black smoke filled the air, the water, and the land with sleeping potion. Everyone fell asleep, sleeping soundly under illusion's blankets. Angel Fires of healing energy appeared to dilute and become incongruent. It appeared that Mother Earth herself had succumbed to death, as even her inhabitants abandoned her.

Smoke is smoke, and now is the moment to clear the smoke screen away. Many of your scholars speak as if the smoke is solid, as if this sleeping potion can have some permanent effect on you. Wake from your sleep, open your eyes, and listen to Us carefully, for We are going to tell you how to clear out the smoke.

We are here to show you, Master Fear is an Angel in disguise.

Master Fear's spell is broken when you remember that abandonment is a figment of Master Fear's imagination. The only cure for abandonment is completely filling the human vessel with Mother Father God's Divine Love. Receiving love from outside your own Self, like from other humans, earthly possessions, or from intellectual pursuits does not substitute for Divine Love. Master Fear would like you to believe that love can only come from outside your Self.

We reveal the secret: Divine Love comes from inside, inside your heart where the riches of your soul, the infinite source of God, lives. We are here to show you the Angel way for opening the source and filling your whole Self with ultimate, complete fulfillment. In the process of allowing yourself to receive Divine Love, the human mind, body, emotions, and spirit gradually let go of the fear of abandonment. As the evolution continues, life becomes more free and joyful, and eventually your outer reality looks, feels, smells, and tastes like paradise. When your vessel is full and your thirst for love is completely satisfied, then, and only then can you fully enjoy loving and receiving love from other humans, earthly possessions, and intellectual pursuits.

Can you imagine your world when every human being lives in this reality, the reality of Heaven on Earth? What would it be like to live in a world where fear does not exist? We are certain you will join in Our mission to cut through the chord holding you captive to Master Fear's illusion.

STEP ONE, FILLING THE VESSEL WITH DIVINE LOVE

We begin. The first step alternates with the second step. There are only two steps to creating miracles. We will ask you to repeat these two steps until every human being is awake, free, and living in peace and harmony. The process takes one moment. We are certain you are ready!*

Go to your kitchen and take a cup from the shelf and hold it with both hands. The God Essence in you helped to manifest this little cup, and this is why it is in your cabinet. Feel the cup and send Love to the cup. Allow the cup to be a representative of you; it is as if the cup is your own child.

Look down on your heart, and feel the organ beat within your chest. Imagine an emerald green gold Light starting to flow out

---

*This imagery is included on the audio CD.

from your heart, and see the Light of Divine Love fill the cup you are holding.

Imagine you then drink the Divine Love into your whole Self and visualize this Light is like your blood, and see it flow into every cell of your entire body. Say inside the words, "I Am one with Mother Father God."

After you become comfortable with drinking Divine Love from your cup, open your imagination and visualize the cup as the child of your heart. Send Divine Love to each other in a rainbow of colors, and say inside, "I Am God's Rainbow of Love and I give my Love to You."

STEP TWO, LETTING GO

Step two is allowing God, Divine Love, to come first in your daily life. We have discovered humans have the best intentions at following step two, and then step two gets lost in abandonment all over again. It is the fear of abandonment that tells you constantly to place others, their responsibilities, their issues, and problems and concerns above those of your own heart.

We ask you to sit with this concept for a moment and ask your Self if this feels like Truth.

To move past the fear of abandonment and allow Divine Love to come first, *it is necessary for you to let go of every person, every possession, and every situation or experience you are afraid of losing*. We call this your journey through the Hell of your attachments.

Once you have faced the fear of losing what you are attached to, the fear is gone, and you will have the thing, person, situation, or experience returned to you, or something even better.

The Twelve Archangels are leading you through your attachments one step at a time. Often, you do not know what you are attached to until the attachment is taken away. Angels are Grim Reapers in that We take away your fears so you can experience your heart's desires and most miraculous dreams-come-true.

We thank you for bravely choosing to assist Us in bringing Heaven and Earth back together.

To take the second step, ask Us to show you, gently, what you are attached to through fear. Our promise is that as you let go of all your Ego tells you that you must control, true Love and eternal freedom will come to you. We remind you, Master Fear is an Angel in disguise. All that Mother Father God requires from you is to face your fears because fear tells your mind not to believe God supplies all you need for your greatest good and evolution. As soon as you become aware of what you are afraid of losing, surrender the fear and know once you face it, the fear no longer exists.

Here is an example of a common human fear: one day, you discover you have an attachment to money. Angels will hold your hands and support you as you travel through the experience of having no money or, to be more accurate, having no money when you expect to have the money. We will help you let go of believing you must have money to survive, and We will help you show yourself that you do not need to compromise your integrity to obtain money.

At the moment of your complete surrender, money will come. The entire experience can take an instant, and when you *allow Our assistance*, the experience of releasing the attachment can be effortless and painless.

Letting go is a process, and often, attachments hide other attachments. When you ask for Our guidance, We will show you how to peel through the attachments at Light speed. Keep breathing, close your eyes, hang on tight, and repeat step one. Before you know it, you will have more of what your heart wants than you have ever dreamed of, and better yet, you will not be afraid of losing it.

Following step one and step two will make your human consciousness expand. As you fill your vessel, it overflows with Divine Love, and with Divine Love comes Divine power.

If you follow Our two steps, We give you our 100 percent guarantee, soon you will have Heaven all around you, and you will know you are equal in Love power to an Archangel.

For Heaven to return, We need YOU! Everyone is called, and the more who come, the faster God's Will will be done on Earth as it is in Heaven.

To know what an Angel knows, sees, and feels and to perform healing miracles like an Angel can do, follow step one and step two.

Blessings and Thank God for *You*!

BOOK THREE

Light and Dark, Where Does Separation Begin and End Inside of You?

Mother Father God created you, the human vessel, as a whole being of spirit, body, thought, and emotion. Each vessel is designed to live in complete Oneness with all other vessels and all of Mother Father God's Creation. Inside the human vessel are the four aspects of God:

Mother / emotional body
Father / mental body
Divine Love / spiritual body
Creation / physical body.

Each aspect or body of the vessel is created to be inseparable from the other. When the bodies are in balance and anchored in God's

Sound and Light, the vessel, the human Self can only experience a reality of Heaven, perfect joy, peace, harmony, and Oneness. Because your human vessel is one with all other human vessels, when your bodies are completely balanced, you create an infinitely powerful force of Divine Love that pulls all other vessels into balance.

Fear creates a disturbance in the mental body, causing an illusionary perception of separation between the mental, emotional, physical, and spiritual bodies. When your mental body is free of fear, your four bodies will return to their natural state of balance. As you do this, all of humanity shall return to a divine state of freedom and inner wholeness.

We, the Twelve Archangel Kingdoms of the Central Sun, welcome you to experience an integration of your thought and feeling, your mind with your spirit and body, as you have never considered to be possible here on Earth. We ask you to find your courage and know as you choose to walk through fear's illusions into Divine Light, you open doorway after doorway for all whom you love.

We tell you a mystery, and We hope perhaps you will be the one to accept the miracle of courage. In truth, to bring Heaven and Earth together in Divine Union takes only one human vessel. We need one human being brave enough to fight for freedom for your entire human race. You see, bright Child of God, Master Fear has tricked you into believing the journey is impossible, that you do not have the strength or the willpower to set your vessel free. We know how wise you are becoming, and so We ask you to walk together with Us. We will take you home, and you will never feel alone again.

We begin by describing to you the different parts of the human vessel, and We will tell you how separation between the human and Mother Father God is perpetuated with each part. We will teach you how to heal the separation by reaching deeper and deeper into your Light; as you transform and become one with God consciously, you help all humanity awaken to Heaven.

Heaven is the home of God, and the home of God is found inside your loving heart. We thank you for bringing Heaven and Earth together. We thank you for creating miracles for your Self and those you love.

PART ONE: THE SPIRITUAL BODY

The spiritual body is your body of Light and Sound. This Energy Body holds the human soul, God's Energy existing on the physical earth dimension, together with the

OverSoul, God's Energy existing in the dimensions of Heaven. Perhaps you can imagine your spiritual body as the embryonic sac surrounding and nurturing your whole vessel. The sac feeds you with God's Light and Sound as your mental, emotional, and physical Self expands, evolves, and rebalances back to a state of Oneness.

The spiritual body provides God's Energy to you through the chakras, the energy centers of the human vessel. These energy centers supply Divine Love to all the parts of your physical body as well as give support to your mental body and to your emotional body. Held within the chakras is the memory of all your experiences on Earth this life or any life, past or future, as well as parallel lives in other worlds of the great Cosmos.

You have the ability to communicate with your chakras through your intuition at all times. Intuition is the channel between your spiritual body and your mental body. The Body of Sound and Light is constantly sending you messages through the subtle thoughts of your intuitive mind. We are willing to teach you how to hear the voice of your intuition by opening and transforming your mental body. When the thinking mind is clear, you will hear your intuitive thoughts and know they are God's Truth.

PART TWO:
THE MENTAL BODY

The mental body is your thinking mind, all the multitude of thoughts passing through your brain at any given moment. Some thoughts catch your attention, and you consciously hear their message. Other thoughts drift by and stay in the background, so quiet or buried you may miss their messages entirely. Thoughts are messengers between the mental, spiritual, emotional, and physical bodies.

The mind is similar to a television with the ability to receive a variety of different stations or channels. When the mind's TV is turned on, you can listen and see the current program running through your consciousness. You can think of the TV as your conscious awareness, thoughts you are paying attention to. Your mental TV set can have many stations, yet the viewer typically watches one station or channel at a time.

For you to "tune into" your physical Self, your mind turns to the physical body channel on the TV. When you wish to understand the depth of your emotions, the mind selects the appropriate channel for your emotional body. A channel requiring special reception on the TV is the intuition channel which relays programs from your spiritual body. Angels use the intuition channel to communicate with you. As you open to receiving Our Love, it becomes easier for you to tune your mental TV to your intuitive thoughts. Intuitive thoughts coming from your spiritual body broadcast news and information giving clarity and insight into your mental, emotional, and physical bodies as well as news concerning other human beings and God's Creation.

Intuitive thought is pure, simple, and quiet compared with the authoritative distracting thoughts of the Ego. Angels describe the human Ego as your personality. The Ego decides how you identify your Self in the world in relation to other people. A free and integrated Ego defers authority to the intuition. When this great union between the conscious awareness and intuition happens, the human knows and trusts he or she is a Child of God and worthy of total freedom.

We are here to help you guide your Ego back to a place of Oneness with your spiritual Self. To do this, you need to transform all conscious thoughts giving the message you are still separate or unworthy. Fear tells the Ego through conscious and subconscious thought patterns to believe only the practical, rational, and tangible.

We wish to describe four important thought patterns generated by fear that enable the Ego to stay apart from your spiritual Self and the intuitive voice. These thought patterns keep fear alive in your mental, emotional, and physical bodies.

WANTING. "Wanting" thoughts constantly tell you what you want that you do not have in the time and space your Ego demands.

CONTROLLING. "Controlling" thoughts suggest what action you must force from your Self or another to get what your Ego wants when and where it wants it.

COMPARING. "Comparing" thoughts tell you to compare your earthly accomplishments, physical beauty, emotional status, and mental intelligence with other human beings. Comparing thoughts place your Ego in competition with all other Egos.

JUDGING. Last are the "judging" thoughts. Judging thoughts often follow comparing thoughts. They evaluate where you are according to the Ego's list of standards and expectations for your progress through life.

We will show you how to transform these thought patterns by clearing your mental body with Mother Father God's Divine Love. Fearful thought patterns must be cleared again and again until the mind no longer reacts to them. As the conscious thoughts are cleared, the subconscious thoughts and memories from your past surface and clear. During this cyclical process, the unconscious transforms into an instinctual state of trust and unity with all of God's Creation.

The unconscious includes concepts you live by that you have no memory of; it is just what you have always done and have always believed about your Self, life, your world, and your relationship to God. As transformation of fearful thought patterns proceeds, the human mind develops and begins to believe miracles are possible, and the Ego is integrated with your heart. When the Ego and the intuitive voice of your heart become one voice, your conscious awareness is always and forever tuned into your purest Truth. God's Love and power become the unconscious mind, and trusting God's plan becomes a way of life.

Because each human mind is influenced by all other minds, your transformation is connected to the transformation of all other people. As your mind becomes free, you help all human beings break free from the bonds of Master Fear's slavery. It is only a moment away when all human minds will complement and work synergistically together. Your integrated Ego will allow God's purpose for you and all you know to manifest on Earth. Believe that you deserve to live in a world where each human being feels completely satisfied and works in harmony with all living creatures.

PART THREE:
THE EMOTIONAL BODY

Emotion, when allowed to flow free and pure, is Mother God's Holy Spirit. Holy Spirit is unconditional Love, the almighty healing force and cure for all human dysfunction. Feelings are messages generated by the mental body identifying where emotion is blocked or moving freely within the vessel. Joy is a manifestation of feeling Holy Spirit freely within the human Self. Sadness, guilt, depression, loneliness, and holding your breath are messages telling you to clear more anger.

Anger is blocked Holy Spirit. When the mind identifies the feeling of anger, the vessel breathes and releases the anger and unlocks the force of emotion to open and heal the heart, mind, and body. Angels see anger as a most positive feeling, for it is anger that can show you the door to freedom. At the primal level, human beings are angry that Mother Father God abandoned them. Clearing anger from your vessel opens the river of Divine Love in your heart. Love flows into your awareness thought by thought and experience by experience and transforms fear wherever Love finds it.

You ask Us about the feeling called "fear." We tell you, humans can *think* fear, and you can experience the results of this thought; however, it is impossible for you to experience fear as an emotion. When the mind — whether in the unconscious, subconscious, or conscious state — releases or produces fearful thoughts, the heart closes, the Holy Spirit is blocked, and the physical body responds by some form of trauma. This shock can be felt as numbness, pain, or panic. When you remember with your whole mind that nothing in your world can create or destroy you for you are God's Energy, you are free from fear.

As you become free from fear, the Holy Spirit, Mother God's pure unconditional Love, fills your inner and outer world, and it is no longer possible for you and the human family to experience fear. Listen to your feelings from your Center with your intuitive mind, for these intuitive thoughts will tell you where you still block the Holy Breath. Opening your heart and centering your mind allows Emotion to flow. This allowing of feeling your emotion, quietly and privately in your own sacred space, will heal you completely and bring you back to Oneness forever.

PART FOUR: THE PHYSICAL BODY

The physical body is the absorbent sponge for fear from the mental body. The physical body absorbs repressed emotion, and together mental fear and emotional repression create imbalance, pain, and illness in the physical body. The physical is usually the last body to heal from the effects of fear. Angels have physical bodies made of Light and Music. It is Our desire to help you remember how to lighten yourselves so your energy can flow and set you free. Athletes understand how to move their life force freely in their bones and flesh so that they become more flexible, faster and more graceful. Imagine the athlete breathing in the Holy Spirit so Emotion is free to unlock the vessel from fear. Imagine this athlete thinking, "Love is who I Am."

With a little practice, the human is as free as an Angel. Perhaps you were born with a physical body that remains stiff and slow to move. When you use your imagination and your emotion to see, feel, and believe that your physical body is free, you help Us free all humankind. Humans often feel their physical body holds them in like a prison. We are asked, "How can my Divine Essence fit into this one small physical container?" We are telling you how to stretch and how to open your physical body so God's Light and Sound can send you flying by expanding what appears to be compact and dense. Your physical body is the sacred temple of God, and the temple needs to be cared for as you would care for the most expensive, precious material possession you own.

Remembering that you have a physical body is not always easy for human beings. Often you are living in the future your mental body is picturing for you. We ask you to ask your own Guardian Angels and your own intuitive voice to simply remind you to notice the house you are living in, your body. When you remember your body, picture yourself moving and allow space in your day for moving. It is not so important how you move, whether you dance, walk, jog, or swim. All that matters is for you to help the energy generated by your chakras to move. We recommend you do this with thought, feeling, and action. The human being is a spiritual vessel containing God's Energy in thought (the mental body), in emotion (the emotional body), and in movement and form (the physical body).

CREATING ONENESS WITHIN THE HUMAN VESSEL

Transformation and integration together make an incredible journey of evolution for the human Self. We ask you to seek courage in the moment and focus on your process and progress moment by moment. When you do this, the mental body gradually lets go of time, and the human moves at Light speed on the path home to total freedom. Many teachers and healers are available to you, and We ask you to continue to seek the teacher and healer inside your Self. The teacher is your intuitive channel connecting your spiritual body to your conscious thought. The healer is the unencumbered force of the Holy Spirit called your emotion.

The key to creating Oneness is to consciously will to transform each and every fearful thought in your entire mental body. As you transform the fear in your mental Self — unconscious, subconscious, and conscious — you must will to clear fear from your emotional and physical bodies as well. Your own will is all you need to set you free. We do not promise you an easy path, yet We say it can be effortless if you allow it. Thought by thought, cell by cell, atom by atom, vibration by vibration, you must will to transform the fear hiding in your vessel by believing God is in charge.

Your very own OverSoul is directing your journey through the great schoolroom of Earth. When you ask your Angels to show you how every experience in your life is for your greatest good, you learn how to once again take responsibility back for your life and for your creation. As this happens, you begin to see your Self as the master of your life, and all your heart desires begin to flow into your reality, the reality you are consciously creating.

We present you with the Angel Keys to human freedom. Can you achieve this freedom this lifetime? It is entirely up to you and how willing you are to open. Please understand, God asks you to be willing, and willing does not mean you walk your journey alone. Willingness is an intention from your heart. At times, your mind will close again, but it will open when you choose to surrender. Surrendering to Mother Father God is allowing your Self to see the Truth in what is happening to you. It is refusing to believe you are a victim of circumstance, and it is the development of great tolerance and patience for your Self for not learning as fast as your Ego believes you should.

Freedom takes longer than the blink of an eye or snap of the fingers. Freedom requires you to heal the separation between you and your OverSoul, between you and God, layer by layer of misconception. We remind you that you have manifested into many atoms, cells, thoughts, feelings, and concepts about what is real. You must know. You must forgive. You must allow your whole vessel to be one with God forever.

We, the Twelve Archangels of The Central Soul, present you

OUR ANGEL KEYS TO FREEDOM OF THE HUMAN VESSEL

1) *Be willing and say often, "I Am the Will of God."*

2) *Be willing to take responsibility for every thought, feeling, and experience in your life*, both joyful and painful. We ask you to say often, " I Am my highest joy and good."

3) *Demand to see the gift in all your experiences*, even the most tragic. Ask your intuitive channel, "What does this teach me?" "How does this help my heart to open?" "How is this for my greatest good?"

4) *Listen to your anger* for your anger shows you where the Holy Spirit, the Divine force of emotion, is blocked inside you. We ask you to say often, "I Am releasing and I Am free."

5) *Remember time is an illusion that desires to trap you into fear again*. Masters and human beings never go backwards on their

path home to God. The journey takes just the right amount of time, and you are moving at just the right speed for your vessel.

6) *Ask for the miracle of balance between all the bodies in your vessel.* Be willing to ask for assistance in correcting imbalance wherever you discover it. We are always available, and when you need earthly help, We will help you find a healer who can assist in your rebalancing. We ask you to say, "I Am willing to experience the miracle of balance."

We give you a shortcut* to doing all the above, as Angels believe in efficiency. Work with God's Energy, as you are energy and you are one with God.

USING GOD'S ENERGY TO CLEAR THE ENTIRE MENTAL BODY (MENTAL AURA): *Imagine the following, and We ask you to remember you are welcome to change the imagery. Our visualizations are all metaphorical in that all Angel Fire is a pure vibration of Divine Love. Visualize yourself holding Archangel Michael's sword of sapphire-blue Fire. This is the Light of Truth and God's Will. Take the sword and quickly slice off your head from the base of your neck up. Imagine your head lands quite gently into a boiling pot of Violet Fire,*

---

*This imagery is included on the audio CD.

God's Energy of Transformation and Forgiveness. Breathe and say inside, "I Am Love." Do this when your mind is obsessing over the future or when negative thoughts are traveling through your awareness.

USING GOD'S ENERGY TO CLEAR THE EMOTIONAL BODY (EMOTIONAL AURA): *Imagine you are sitting in a large, round room with the lights off. Turn on the lights and look for any images that make you feel uncomfortable. We have observed many humans finding monsters, weapons, dark clouds, dying people, hissing snakes, and barbed wire in their emotional space. Visualize a shower of brilliant Violet Fire pouring in from the ceiling and swirling all around the room. Hold the image of violet Light until you see or feel or know the color white, gold or pink. Go further until the round walls of the room are entirely gone and you have become the white, gold, or pink Light of Divine Love. Say the words inside, "I Am free. I Am God, fully human, and I Am human, fully God."*

USING GOD'S ENERGY TO STRETCH AND EXPAND THE PHYSICAL BODY: *Visualize your physical body stretching very long and very wide. Breathe in deeply, and exhale slowly. Imagine yourself stretching all the body parts you can think of; it is like you are looking in different circus mirrors, stretching and breathing. Now* *imagine you are dancing and flying freely in an open space filled with emerald green Light and coral Light. You can climb a mountain and swim across the sea, and you can run faster than an antelope, and you can move your body in any direction you delight in. Say inside, "I Am God, fully human. I Am human, fully God."*

These exercises will work even if you do not see anything; just breathe, and have the desire to clear your mental and emotional auras. Clear them whenever you remember, and you will be doing this just as you need for your highest joy and greatest good. We invite you to visualize clearing the mental and emotional auras for those you love by simply picturing your loved one standing in the healing Light.

BOOK FOUR

Angel Power Tools, Working with the God Force of the Chakras

Human beings have all the magic they need to create miracles every moment of their existence on Earth. Mother Father God's miraculous power is available to you through the energy centers/chakras of your own spiritual body. Your Guardian Angels fuse Their power with yours to facilitate the creation of just the miracle you need for the greatest good of all concerned. Angel Power Tools are created from God's Light and Sound and the energy (visualized by the color) from your chakras. Our Power Tools merge Divine Love from Heaven with your vessel on Earth. Together, We bring Heaven and Earth together to create miracles in abundance.

Miracles are gifts of Mother Father God's Divine grace. They happen in the moment and always when you need them for your highest joy and greatest good. As you open your mind and become more aware of what your experiences are showing you about your Self, you might just begin to discover miracles happening all the time. Miracles require trust in God's Divine plan and believing that all your experiences are designed to help you break free from fear's limitations.

When you ask God for a miracle, know God always comes through in God's time and in God's way. Angels specialize in seeing the big picture. We can see how manifesting your request affects all of humanity. Often, We are called to orchestrate and synchronize miracles so all God's Creation benefits from each gift of Divine grace.

Angel Power Tools, intention, imagery and affirmations are used for opening your awareness to perceive God's incredible, amazing magic happening for you exactly when you need it most. Our Power Tools come in handy for helping those you love and those you dislike. Angel Energy follows God's Laws and can only be used for the greatest good of all. We invite you to play with our Angel Fires and use your imagination to invent new tools for waking up humanity. Every human being has equal potential for opening and receiving the infinite Love and abundant wealth of the Great Cosmos. All people can live in peace, plenty, good health, and continuous joy.

We, The Twelve Archangels of the Central Sun, show you how!

INSTRUCTION BOOKLET FOR ANGEL FIRE POWER TOOLS

CONNECTING TO THE POWER SUPPLY OF THE CHAKRAS

Your spiritual body is filled with energy centers supplying Divine Love to all the components of your mental, emotional, and physical bodies. When these energy centers are open, all of this miraculous God power is available to you to use to set yourself free from fear. This energy is also available to you to help all of God's Creation on planet Earth and beyond. To use any of the Angel Power Tools, all you need to do is be willing to open the appropriate chakra. *Doing the visualizations of the Angel imagery (Power Tools) automatically opens and clears all the chakras of your entire vessel, especially the third-eye chakra located in the middle of your forehead. This chakra is the power source for your intuition channel, connecting your spiritual body to the conscious thoughts and images of your mental body. The more you use this chakra, the more available and clearer your intuitive voice becomes.*

Angel Power Tools include what could be seen as violent weapons. When a human being is hurt, it is natural instinct to want to hurt back. Using the Power Tools actually raises the instinctual vibration of violence into that of volitional, positive action. The auras are cleared instantly, and usually the participant is left feeling peaceful with new clarity and forgiveness.

POWER TOOLS OF LOVE

VIOLET FIRE, TRANSFORMATION AND FORGIVENESS, CROWN CHAKRA

Violet Fire comes from your crown chakra. The crown chakra is located at the top of your head and is responsible for supplying your mental body with pure Divine Thought Energy from Father God.

Violet Fire is extremely thorough at erasing fearful thoughts and changing fear back into love. Here are some Violet Fire Power Tools and their suggested use.

VIOLET FIRE GRENADES AND FIREBALLS Close your eyes, and imagine you have a whole basket of Violet Fire grenades or fireballs. Pull the pin on the grenades, and throw them at anyone you like, including yourself. See the person, past experience, or other object of interest explode in a beautiful violet Light and take a deep breath. Angels explode planet Earth in Violet Fire several times a day in order to help transform the fear generated by human thought. The metaphor for Violet Fire grenades, fireballs, ray guns, and Love bombs is *Instant Transformation*.

Healing Exercise: Blow up any scenes from your childhood or past, addictive substances, people you need to forgive, or political situations on your planet needing to be released and transformed into love and peace. Say inside, "I Am releasing and I Am forgiving." Visualize new scenes for the little child in your heart, and create a new past of love and Oneness with your family of choice and Guardian Angels. Visualize a new world where everyone lives in peace, harmony, and abundance. Violet Fire is Mother Father God's miraculous alchemical Light. Use it, and We fuse Our Light with your Light. Create a new present and future by transforming the old fearful energy of the past!

VIOLET FIRE FUNERAL Violet Fire funerals work splendidly for situations requiring release, forgiveness, and rebirth. You can fill a Violet Fire coffin with your old Self, inhibitions, fears, and even addictions. After the coffin lid is closed, call on Gabriel, Michael, and your Guardian Angels, and roll the violet coffin into the white Light crematorium. Breathe and say inside, "I Am free." It is very cleansing to imagine your Self lying in the purple Light and imagining your whole body exploding and dissolving in the white Light of Divine Love. Violet Fire funerals are very helpful for clearing attachments from past relationships.

VIOLET FIRE WATERFALL AND VIOLET SWIMMING POOL The Violet Fire waterfall is a most joyful and calming experience and works well for those who have difficulty with visual imagery. We suggest you turn your daily shower into a violet waterfall of God's Light. As the water falls on your head, allow all your fearful and negative thoughts and doubts, all old emotional baggage, and any physical discomforts to be gently cleansed away. The Violet Fire transforms all the "dirt" into Love and Oneness with your heart Center. You can even imagine all the *shabungi* (toxic waste produced from fear) going down the drain. Where does it go? All thought is God's Energy, and so the shabungi is transformed back into Divine Love and returned to your own crown chakra. The energy is now sacred and highly charged and actually helps boost your immunity from fear on all levels in all bodies!

Swimming in a Violet Fire-filled pool of Light is nurturing and healing to your human soul. As you imagine you dive into the beautiful purple Light, know that all the experiences you have lived in any lifetime are being transmuted and neutralized. In your visualization, do not be afraid if the Light of the pool turns dark. The darkness comes from your own shadow, the separation between your head and your heart Center, and it is being transformed by the Violet Fire. Visiting the Violet Fire pool is helpful for detoxing the entire vessel of illusions and imprisonments of the outer world.

VIOLET FIRE HELMET When you visualize a Violet Fire helmet on your head, you will discover that your worries and Self-doubt are erased from your conscious thoughts. The helmet works by opening up your own crown chakra and filling your brain cells with God's Divine Love in the form of crystal clear Divine Thought. Because you cannot think from a position of love and fear at the same moment, fear is cleared away.

This Angel helmet works extremely well for calming obsessive and compulsive anxiety and negative thinking about the future. We recommend that students wear their helmet for all exams, presentations, and interview situations because when you are clear, you can create a joyful learning and remembering experience. All knowledge is already inside of you, and wearing the helmet helps your brain to open so you can retrieve what you need.

VIOLET FIRE ERASER AND MAGIC BLACKBOARD

Stored within your subconscious and unconscious memories are concepts about yourself, humanity and reality needing to be transformed. For example, you or someone in your family may have the concept that someone with your last name is entitled to experience hardship on the earth. Perhaps because your mother died of cancer, you have a buried belief that you are to die of cancer too. When such a concept of separation between you and total freedom surfaces, imagine yourself writing the concept down on the magic blackboard.

Take a deep breath, and visualize erasing the concept, written in the form of A=B (surname=hardship or mother=me) with a brilliantly bright Violet Fire eraser. Say the words inside, "I release and I Am free." Open your eyes, and state your new belief out loud to your Self.

BOILING VIOLET FIRE SULFURIC ACID We recommend you use the imagery of boiling Violet Fire sulfuric acid on your toughest situations. If you or someone you know is struggling with deep-seated victim consciousness, you can ask the Twelve Archangels to boil you or that person in a special vibration of Violet Fire. This vibration is very high and comes from the crown chakra of Mother Father God's Center, or the Central Soul. Boiling Violet Fire sulfuric acid is metaphorical for the complete dissolving of the mental body of all fear from any lifetime. When you ask for someone or a situation to be boiled in this energy, your mental body is automatically transmuted as well. Because of the extremely pure and powerful form of Violet Fire, transformation and integration are rapid and penetrating.

When the process is complete, the person is then placed into the white gold Light of Divine Love for neutralization and recovery. The Twelve Archangel Kingdoms work with your OverSoul to facilitate this powerful healing of the human mental body. Although boiling Violet Fire sulfuric acid sounds deadly, We remind you God's Energy can only be used for the greatest good and highest joy of all concerned. Sometimes fear is deep and dark for it has condensed into evil, cruelty, and hatred. We present you with God's formula for even the toughest fear; use it with an open heart and an awake mind!

HOLY SPIRIT, RED FIRE OF UNCONDITIONAL LOVE AND COMPASSION, ROOT CHAKRA

Holy Spirit is Mother God's unconditional Love Energy of pure Emotion. This Energy is supplied to you from your root chakra located at the base of your spine. This energy center grounds you to Mother Earth so you can receive all the material resources you need to live on Earth in a healthy body. When this chakra is open and fully functioning, the human has no fear of death or abandonment.

Working with the Angel Holy Spirit Power Tools allows you to clear away blocked emotion, insecurity, and low self-esteem. Mother God's Love is soothing, nurtures and heals the little child inside your heart, and brings peace to your mind and relaxation to your body. Holy Spirit is pure unconditional Mother's Love available to you at all times to help you live your highest and most joyful destiny on Earth.

HOLY SPIRIT (RUBY PINK) LIGHT JACUZZI BUBBLE BATH The unconditional Love of Mother God merged with the abundant Love from Mother Earth creates an experience you can feel with your physical body as well as your emotional and mental bodies. Come, and imagine your Self and the child of your heart joyfully playing in the pink Light bubble bath. Soak up the pink Light of Mother Love, and allow all your insecurities and stress from the day to melt away. Take in some deep, slow breaths and exhale slowly and completely. Say inside, "I Am receiving Love."

FUZZY PINK LIGHT BLANKET, SLIPPERS AND PACIFIER/BABY BOTTLE Angel blankets gently calm down the most savage beast. We invite you to wrap yourself or someone you know who needs affection in a Holy Spirit pink blanket. See yourself snuggled up from head to toe, and breathe in the nurturing comfort of the pink Light.

If you know of someone who is in a rage or in a place of great fear or dark negativity, imagine a little child inside with a pink Light pacifier or drinking from a pink baby bottle filled with ruby pink Light. Mother God's Love united with Mother Earth's physical reassurance will have your loved one feeling better instantly. Everyone needs mothering affection and attention. We welcome you to bring in Holy Spirit, an inexhaustible source of full-time Mother's Love!

VISITING THE HOLY GRAIL Archangel Raphael welcomes you to join her for a swim in God's cup of overflowing healing Love. The Holy Grail is a sacred bowl made of gold Light of Divine Love and filled with ruby pink Holy Spirit. This pink Light vibrates at a special frequency, as it shares both Mother God's unconditional Love and Divine Love's deep healing power of the human soul. Imagine you and any hurting, sexually or physically abused faces of your Self diving into the Great Golden Cup; know as you move through the Light, every particle of God's Energy that is you is cleansed and made new.

Every atom of your physical, mental, and emotional body is recreated and cleared of all trauma your vessel is ready to release.

If you are a healer of others, We hope you will bring your patients to Raphael's sanctuary. You need never fear you are trespassing another's boundaries by visualizing others in Holy Spirit. If it is for their greatest good, their own OverSoul hears your request and brings them to the sanctuary. You are acting as a messenger from a place of love and compassion.

HOLY SPIRIT I. V., INTRA-VESSEL RECHARGE When you or someone you know is feeling clingy and excessively dependent and needing of attention, ask your Angels to hook you or your loved one up to the Holy Spirit I. V.. Holy Spirit from the Center of Mother Father God, Divine Love and Creation is sent directly into the root chakra and recharges this energy center. As this chakra is refueled, the human receives Love from both Earth and Heaven and begins to feel self-sufficient and independent.

If you are called to give attention, affection, and acknowledgment to the point where you are feeling drained by others, it is critical for you to refuel before you collapse physically. Recharging the root chakra with the Holy Spirit I. V. boosts your immune system and can speed your recovery if you are ill. To hook up, close your eyes, breathe, and say inside, "I allow God's Love to flow into my root chakra, and I give thanks this is so now."

RIDING THE RED HORSE OF EMOTIONAL POWER

Mother God's Energy of Emotion can work like dynamite to blast open blockages preventing your whole Self from feeling your feelings and from understanding what your feelings are telling you. Remember, feelings are actually mental messages identifying where emotional energy is blocked or opening in your vessel. When it benefits your growth to know how the blocks were created, you will remember. If it is not for your greatest good to remember, the blockage is cleared without engaging your conscious awareness.

Riding the scarlet Red Horse of Emotion is an extremely powerful experience, which has the potential of greatly freeing your emotional body. Divine Law allows you to visualize only your Self riding the Red Horse because if you have the desire, then your consciousness is ready. This is not a decision you are allowed to make for another human being.

To ride the Red Horse of Emotion, close your eyes, breathe in deeply, and exhale slowly until you feel centered. Say inside, "I Am calling the Red Horse to me now." Visualize your Self climbing up on the horse's back (you may need your Angel to lift you up). Hang on tight and make toning sounds if you like. The Red Horse knows how long a ride you are ready for; when the ride is complete, you will find your Self fully awake, present, and aware of your surroundings.

ARCHANGEL MICHAEL'S SAPPHIRE-BLUE FLAME OF TRUTH AND WILL, THE THROAT (WILL) CHAKRA

The power of God's Will and Truth comes from the energy center located in the throat area. When this energy center is open, your conscious awareness is connected with your heart, and you are living your purest Truth and communicating this Truth in thoughts, words, and actions. The Flame of Truth gives your Ego the courage to integrate with your intuitive voice so that you know your purest Truth, speak from your God Center, and act for the greatest good of all.

Purest Truth means the level of awareness where you see each experience as a gift showing you the path home to a state of Oneness with all of God's Creation.

Working with Michael's Fire helps you clear out all the times in your life where you have swallowed your willpower and repressed speaking your Truth. Become united with the Will of God, and live your life on Earth awake and active instead of passive and resistant! Michael's Flame of Truth lights the way to Self-expression and freedom for all who have the courage and might to live their Truth!

ARCHANGEL MICHAEL'S SLAM DUNK Close your eyes, and center your vessel by breathing in deeply and exhaling slowly. Invite Michael to slam his mighty sword of sapphire-blue Light into the top of your head, all the way down through your spinal column, and anchor the sword of God's Will into the earth beneath you. Say inside, "I Am willing to know my Truth, see my Truth, hear my Truth, speak my Truth, and live my Truth according to God's Will for the highest joy and greatest good of all."

Placing Michael's sword of God's Will in your spinal column sends the message to your whole vessel and to all God's Creation that you are ready and willing to receive your freedom and to experience your greatest heavenly destiny here on Earth.

BLUE FIRE ARROWS OF TRUTH When you meet other human beings living in denial of their God potential, visualize yourself shooting a flaming blue Light arrow into their head and into their heart. If you wish to call an addiction to their awareness, shoot the arrows into their root and second chakra (located just below the navel) as well as the head and heart. Say the words inside, "I Am God's Will in action for (their name). The words "I Am" call on the power of their OverSoul to help them see God's Truth in their life.

We say thanks to you for assisting other humans on their path home to freedom, and We remind you that with each arrow you send out, you are firing into your own vessel as well. We invite you to see the reflection of your Self in what you have discovered for your fellow humans. As you bring denial of Self to the Light, humanity awakes!

EMERALD GREEN LIGHT OF HEALING AND LOVE, THE HEART CHAKRA

Giving and receiving love in balance and harmony allow the child inside your heart to heal from any past misconceptions or future disillusionments. Opening the heart chakra is a continuous process and will continue forever like an eternal drum beat. Mother Father God's heart beats with yours, expanding and loving and creating. You were born with the potential for sharing great love with your fellow human beings, and now is the time to achieve this potential for giving and receiving love. As you open your heart, humanity opens, and God's Divine Love pours in, fusing Heaven and Earth together. You are never too old to learn how to receive love, and you are always young enough to give love.

RESTING ON THE EMERALD GREEN FIELD OF MOSS

For your heart to open to give love to your Self and to others, it is essential for you to receive love. The imagery of the green Light blanket of moss helps you to experience receiving love from Mother Earth completely united with the central heart of God. Human beings cannot survive without Love, and they need to receive Love from Mother Earth to feel connected to God, to feel connected to their own Center.

We ask you to visualize relaxing on the most plush, sweetest smelling bed of emerald green moss you can imagine. The sky above is clear and sunny. The white gold Light of Divine Love is flowing over you and into you from above while you receive the green Light from the universal heart chakra from below. Say inside, "I Am receiving Love into my whole vessel, above and below, and from within. I Am opening my heart."

VISITING WITH THE GOD CHILD WITHIN AND DANCING WITH YOUR GUARDIAN ANGELS Your heart chakra is the place inside where you can connect to Heaven at any moment. Imagine you are standing in a brilliantly lit emerald green room, and welcome the immortal Child of God to come and tell you words of wisdom. Laugh and listen, for the Child inside is God and can tell you where you are still pretending to be separate from Heaven's Love and abundance.

God's Child of your heart is happy to bring you your Angels, and together you can solve the problems of the world. She can tell you where love needs to be sent and where you need to allow gentleness into your earthly experiences. Visit your opening heart often, and dance with your Angels. Together you can create joyous magic and music to free all that binds you. *Enjoy!*

ANGEL VITAMINS AND HIGH-ENERGY NUTRITIONAL SUPPLEMENTS, THE SOLAR PLEXUS CHAKRA

The solar plexus chakra is located around your stomach area. This energy center is the supplier of your personal power and self-confidence. When you are "hit" by fear, anxiety, or negativity, you may feel sick to your stomach or experience pain and gas. The solar plexus chakra explodes and releases yellow gold Light of Power whenever you feel insulted, cheated, taken for granted, or criticized.

We recommend you replace the "fuses" of this chakra often by visualizing your Self swallowing yellow gold balls of Light whenever you feel you need an energy boost. Say inside, "I Am all-loving, and I Am using my power for the greatest good of all."

Yellow gold Light comes from your own OverSoul. To fully re-energize, imagine your Self sunbathing comfortably in a gold ball of Light and say inside, "I Am one with God." You can also visualize this ball of Light floating down a yellow gold river to a white gold sea of Divine Love. Breathe and relax and enjoy!

SELF-ESTEEM CLEAN OUT, THE SOUL CHAKRA

The soul chakra is the energy center for your sexual energy, creative energy, and the home of your soul in the human vessel. Fear attacks this chakra with ruthless attention, for here exists the umbilical chord between Earth and Heaven. *When the soul chakra is filled with fear's distortion, the human Self can feel deep unworthiness. No list of achievements can ease the discomfort of not feeling good enough.* The Twelve Archangels of the Central Soul focus much Love and attention on humanity's soul chakra, and We hope you will assist us in Our efforts.

BATTERY REPLACEMENT Ask your Angels to create a new battery for your soul chakra, and ask the Angels to increase the energy output potential. Close your eyes, and say inside, "I Am willing to receive a new soul chakra for the highest joy and greatest good of all concerned." Visualize your Self and all your Angels, including the Nature Angel of your own vessel, assisting you in vacuuming up all the broken pieces of your self-esteem with a Violet Fire vacuum cleaner. Sexual energy, when shared out of fear or control, turns dark and may appear to move like swarming venomous snakes or insects. Clear away all darkness and any images of poisonous snakes you see. Breathe, and keep cleaning until you see a soft coral or orange Light, like a beautiful sunset, appear and expand out. We thank you for your great help in returning worthiness and Self respect to the human race.

Angel Power Tools work with your intention to set your Self free from fear so that you can experience your Divine Destiny. We hope you will add new tools to Ours, and together We will use Mother Father God's Love to change reality for the greatest good of all people. We are making rapid progress in bringing Heaven and Earth together.

Free at last, We celebrate with you!

BOOK FIVE

Healing What Hurts by Learning How to Transform Your Karmic Fate

Often, Angels are accused of not understanding what it feels like to constantly face what you are most afraid of. In truth, We do understand. Suffering hurts, and longing brings more longing. We are here, walking with you, boosting your spirits, and whispering, "We love you and We know you can do it." You see, We too have touched humanity's deepest pain because We experience everything you do. This, Our friends, is the Law of One, and We are always and forever one with you. We know your fears, and We know how to show you the way home to complete and forever freedom. We know We can assist you in seeing Heaven before your eyes as well as inside everyone you meet.

Your Earth was originally designed as a schoolroom where souls could come to experience separation from God. Souls now come to Earth to evolve beyond this illusion by transforming karmic debt. Karma means unfinished business; it is a summary of all lifetimes of all your thoughts, feelings, and actions where you believed fear was more powerful than God's Love. Karmic debts are all the limitations — mental, emotional, and physical — you are experiencing during your life on Earth.

The human soul is made of God's Energy, God's Light and Sound. The Law of Karma requires your soul to return to a place of Oneness with God. With each fearful experience, you leave a bit of your Sound and Light behind, and this Law says you must bring all your Sound and Light back home to your human vessel, transforming all you know and all you believe about your Self.

Clearing your karmic debt requires you to integrate your Ego and Shadow with your heart Center and free your Self from attaching to your limitations.

If you were born with physical birth defects, all that is asked of you is for you to go beyond these defects so they do not stand in the way of your service to humanity. When you do this, either the defects will completely disappear while you are on Earth, or your OverSoul will call you home to Heaven. When you return to Earth, you will have no physical defects. Soon, these two solutions will happen simultaneously, for Heaven and Earth will be one.

Each incarnation, you return to Earth with a fresh start, an opportunity to completely finish all you need to finish. Each lifetime, We are responsible for pointing out to you parts of your soul needing to come home. It is not necessary for you to remember your past lives. Any karma that you need to complete, your OverSoul creates for you this lifetime, beginning with your conception. If in a past life, for example, you sold your family into slavery, you will experience the emotional and mental and physical sensations of separation and abandonment. You will have an opportunity to forgive your Self and learn from the human perspective that separation and abandonment are illusions.

Many courageous souls have returned to Earth, even though they had finished all their karmic lessons. Yes, these souls have already experienced Oneness on Earth, and still they have come back. They may or may not have the knowledge that their karma this lifetime, their experiences of separation from God, are make-believe. Karma is like lovely music being played with all the instruments out of tune.

Many courageous souls have returned to Earth to assist in tuning these instruments. How can human beings have compassion for the suffering of others if they, too, do not experience the ravage, the rape, the destruction, and the illusion of fear? As these souls remember how to bring Love into every thought, feeling, and action of their daily lives, their karma is transformed, and their business is completed.

We hope all humans will believe they are among these courageous souls. Human beings have the potential to transform all the separation inside themselves and complete the service they have returned to do. Tuning instruments is a delicate job and requires a very good listening ear and sense of Truth.

Karma is as karma does, and karma comes around quickly these days. Karma is merely illusion, an extraordinary set of screenplays written for you and by you to show you where you are still living in separation and denial of the God force. Transforming even the most diabolical and cruel lifetimes can be effortless when you are willing. Transformation requires love and service and setting your heart free.

Focus on this life, for this life is the key to all lives past and all lives forward. Tune your instruments for this life, and all the music you compose and play will be lovely and healing and perfect. This life is all you need to understand. Transform all the fearful experiences of this life — just the ones you remember will work quite nicely — and *you shall have no karmic debt*, no unfinished business to attend to.

We have one small exception to the above. As you become free, your heart will naturally yearn to assist others in their freedom. We call this High Karma, where your service to God facilitates the freeing of humanity and the creation of Oneness on Earth. We are delighted to come to the Concert of all the instruments playing in tune, in perfect harmony with one another!

Will it be time for you to die and leave the Earth if all your work is done? We tell you, this is the time for play and celebration. Sit back, relax, and observe as Heaven and Earth fuse and are one again forever.

FORGIVING THIS LIFETIME

Some experience Master Fear's allies of emotional and/or physical abandonment, neglect, and abuse at the moment of conception. Others may experience separation later in infancy, childhood, or adolescence. Why does separation from

Mother Father God happen when the human is so young? The soul enters the human being at conception, coming and going until the baby is ready to be born. Sometimes, the soul changes its mind and decides to come at a later time. Whether this is by natural miscarriage, the mother's choice to stop her pregnancy, or by early death, Divine Order and God's Will are still in charge.

The parents and the newly incarnated soul have agreed to this experience, and We hope all concerned see the return of the new soul as an opportunity for growth and forgiveness. Each birth of a human being happens because the OverSoul has decided to incarnate, to send God's Light and Sound to Earth to learn and facilitate Oneness.

Death and birth are never mistakes or accidents. The soul always knows exactly what it needs to experience. To taste, touch, feel, smell, and know Master Fear is a gift the newly incarnated soul agrees to give to humanity for the expansion and evolution of God. The reward for transforming fear back into love is allowing your vessel to experience forgiveness and love eternal.

Your soul's heart is immune from fear. In your heart, you will find everlasting love in the face and the essence of the God Child within. God Child is a metaphor for the source of Divine Love and the key to forgiving all karmic debt for this life and all lives past and future. This child within your heart has your face and keeps all the memories of your life from time of conception and all knowledge of all experiences until your exit from Earth. Light and Sound are who this Child of God is, and Light and Sound are what this Child is here to bring to you. Abandonment, sorrow, unworthiness, and all other manifestations of separation from Mother Father God and God's Creation cover this Child of Divine Love in a dense, cloudy, and confused vibration. The covering is what many of your scholars refer to as the "inner child."

We present you with how you can delicately, gently, and compassionately raise the vibration of separation belonging to the inner child to the glorious, joyful, and free vibration of the God Child.

First, We need you to acknowledge you have an "inner child," an acknowledgment that you too have experienced feeling abandoned by God at some moment in your childhood or adolescence. We ask you not to compare your childhood with another's childhood. All are equal in the eyes of Mother Father God. Separation is an illusion. Abandonment is an illusion, as is physical, mental, and emotional suffering. This does not mean you did not truly suffer from tragic and trying experiences. It means illusion is not God's Reality and therefore is easy to transform. You will experience and know and understand. As the process continues, all painful and embarrassing childhood memories will no longer have an emotional or mental distressing charge (effect) on your life. The memories will seem like old film footage that has no meaning to who you are and who you are becoming.

Second, We need you to practice the miracle of forgiveness and be willing to remember how to treat your human Self as Mother Father God treats your soul between each incarnation on Earth. Just as you have God's Child living within your heart Center, you also have both a Divine Mother and Divine Father. Your Divine Mother and Father are aspects or faces of your own OverSoul and They, too, can be communicated with at will. As you embrace the child within, your heart opens the doorway between Earth and Heaven. Walk with Us through this door, and your Mother and Father will greet you and take care of you. You are Their only Child.

We hope you will register and participate in the Twelve Archangels of the Central Soul's Reparenting Class. Intend to heal completely and live on Earth as you do in Heaven. We will assist you in uncovering God's Child, and God's Child will introduce you to more of *You*, your Divine Mother and Father. One final step remains, meeting the Nature Angel who gives you life force or "chi" in physical manifestation. United once again, Mother God with

Father God, one with Divine Love together with Creation. Allow your human being to remember his or her infinite worth. Knowing your family inside opens the door to connecting with all God's Family living on your magic planet.

STARTING ALL OVER— REBIRTHING CLASS

What would your life be like if you could start it all over again, conceived in unconditional Love, born into Love, and raised in Love? What would life feel like if you had never been exposed to fear's illusion of being separated from Mother Father God.

We begin by showing you how to gather your soul's Sound and Light lost during conception, gestation, and birth. You are welcome to open your heart and will to do the imagery for your parents as well as for your siblings and children. We thank you for helping Us rebirth humanity into total and complete unconditional Love.

You are welcome to do this visualization again and again and fill your beginning with more Divine Love. Each time you use your will and intention to reconnect with Divine Love at the beginning of this incarnation, We promise you will experience greater freedom and mobility in your daily life. Each time you melt away the misconception that fear can influence how you live, who you are, and what you believe, you erase the effects of fear's negativity from your genetic coding. As the genetic code changes, you once again have a cellular, unconscious trust that Mother Father God supports you totally. When the unconscious trusts, the subconscious and the conscious follow, love fills your thoughts, and loving-kindness becomes your natural behavior.

VISUALIZATION*

Close your eyes, breathe in gentle and deep relaxed breaths, and breathe out completely.

Say inside, "I Am one with Mother Father God."

Allow your hands to become God's hands, and breathe.

Open your hands, and allow the chakras in the center of your palms to relax. They will open and begin to pulse with Divine Love.

Into these hands, We place two cells of Light and Sound, one female and one male.

*This imagery is included on the audio CD.

Love these two cells, breathe, and say inside, "I Am one with Mother Father God."

The cells multiply, and the Light and Sound grow. Keep loving these precious cells of God's Energy.

Into these cells a brilliant white gold Light comes, your human soul. Breathe and feel your hands pulse with Love.

The bundle of cells and soul unite and become one. Hold this life in your hands, one with the hands of God.

Feel the fetus grow in these hands, breathe, and love this fetus. The fetus feeds on Divine Love pulsing from your hands and develops into a perfect expression of God's Creation.

At the moment you feel your baby is ready to be born, take your hands holding God's Infant, and birth your new Self into your heart.

Place your hands on your heart, and say inside, "We are one with Mother Father God. I Am born anew in pure and total Divine Love."

Listen to your music, and breathe.

Feel your Guardian Angels holding you, loving you, and healing you.

We are one.

TRANSFORMING THE PAST, LAYER BY LAYER— FORGIVENESS CLASS

Inside every human being is an innocent child, the child who trusts that his or her soul is really immortal and Mother Father God is True and Loving.

Layer by layer of separation between you and Oneness with God and God's Creation has been deposited on your fiery soul. The innocent child within your heart, the child you may not even remember, begins to become lost in the fight to find a place in life on Earth. Gradually, the outer chaos of the visible and tangible world takes over, and life becomes one reaction after another.

When your soul chose your Earth family, you agreed to wear their layers of separation as well as those created from your own experiences. Whether this is your biological family or adoptive family, you agreed to believe in many of the family's concepts about how the world operates and how you are expected to function in this world. Before you were even born, you accepted your family's programming of caretaking of your physical, mental, and emotional bodies and you agreed to transform all neglect, denial, and fear contributing to this programming.

Life, since the moment of your birth, has been showing you what you believe about your Self and how you need to change these limitations and set your soul free again. As you do this for your Self, you set your family of origin free as well.

The process of transformation is complete when you are no longer living in your past or attached and reacting to any experience in your present.

We invite you to look at all situations you find your Self reacting to and ask the question, "Does this feel familiar to me? Have I been here before?" We ask you to go back to your childhood, as far back as you can go and in as deep as your psyche will allow. Far and deep, and here is where you release, transform, and forgive.

Subconscious memories, memories from your past will surface up to your conscious awareness, and here you can use your imagination to work with Our Power Tools to set the child in your heart free. As the subconscious clears, the unconscious cellular memories rise to the subconscious and may begin to show up in your dreams. With continued gentleness and patience, these cellular memories will surface to your conscious awareness, so again you can use your imagination to clear away each layer of separation between you and God.

We ask you to say often, "I Am one with God."

We offer both a visualization for those who enjoy their imagination and a physical/emotional exercise for those who prefer working with feeling and for whom imagery is difficult. *For all Our Power Tools, inner vision is not required, just intention to heal and free your vessel from fear. Know you are working with God's Energy in the way that is for your greatest good!*

VISUALIZATION*— INTENTION FOR FREEING GOD'S CHILD

Close your eyes, and imagine you enter your heart chakra.

The room is emerald green and open. Say inside, "I Am opening." Look in the room for your little child. Is she hiding and bruised? Is he ready to embrace you?

With all your will, send Love to your child and ask for forgiveness. Shower your child with Violet Fire to begin to wash away the separation between you.

---

*This imagery is included on the audio CD.

Ask this child to bring you all your hurting faces from your entire past, even faces of your adult Self. Bring these parts of you home into your heart. Shower each one with violet Light and say inside, "We are one with God. I Am home again."

Allow God's Child to be the guide of your life, and begin by traveling to your past. With each scene that appears on your mental screen, throw a Violet Fire grenade or fireball and say inside, "I Am releasing. I Am transforming. I Am forgiving." Together with your child, change the scene to the way you would have liked, obeying God's Law for the greatest good of all concerned.

Ask your Guardian Angels to show you where you gave your power over to fear when you were a child, an adolescent, young adult, and adult. Go back, take back your power, and know you are one with God.

Ask your child to show you where you learned to devalue your human Self, where you bought fear's illusion that humans are less than God. Say inside, "I Am God, fully human. I Am human, fully God."

You see, you are worthy of comfort, security, affection, abundance, and happiness. We thank you for remembering your worthiness and claiming what is yours.

As you transform your past, you transform your future, for you are the creator of your reality. Be brave, and transform the old programming on behalf of yourself and the human race. You deserve to live life on Earth as you do in Heaven.

The God Child is free when you remember with each thought, feeling, and physical movement to allow your heart to guide you and return you to a place of innocent trust.

Every painful experience is a miraculous gift to show you where the old programming is still inhibiting your freedom. *Fight for your life!* Remember, many brave souls have returned to liberate humanity so all can live freely, so all can live in Oneness with God's Creation.

DANCING WITH YOUR HEART, NON-VISUAL EXERCISE

(Music or Nature Required)

If an outdoor sacred place is available to you, We invite you to go to that place, take off your shoes, and begin to walk in a circle.

Your circle has a starting point; walk your circle. Try to feel the ground beneath your feet as if you were doing this for the very first time.

Walk faster until you are dancing, moving your arms in all directions without purpose or agenda. Look at the scenery around you as if you were seeing it for the first time.

Sing if you like. We ask you to sing about love and about the child that is you.

If you prefer indoors, play your favorite music as loud as is comfortable for you. It is important for you to feel the vibration of the sound.

Lie down, stretch, and send love to any tight place or place in pain. Begin to rock your body, and either hug yourself or place your hands on your heart. Rock as fast as you can and sound out any sounds or words coming to you.

Breathe and stand up, stretch, and move.

Move as if you have just been released from a mummy suit.

Stand under a warm, bright light or stand in the sunshine. Feel the sound and the warmth of the light as if you were doing this for the first time. Say, "I love you." Again and again.

We invite you to try all exercises for connecting with your heart and healing the separation between you and God. We are hopeful you will find Our exercises so delightful you will do them again and again and create new ones just for your beautiful child within your heart!

MAKING ROOM FOR MOM AND DAD— DIVINE FEMALE AND MALE CLASS

To assist you in healing the separation between Heaven and Earth inside your human vessel, We recommend you invite your Divine Mother and Divine Father into your conscious awareness. These Divine Parents teach you how to parent your human Self with total, full-time, unconditional Love and support.

The heart chakra is a doorway between Earth and Heaven. When you walk through this door with your intention, you can connect with the male and female energies of your OverSoul. As you open to the energy of your Divine Male, the vibration of your thoughts begins to shift from fear-based to love-based. Connecting with your Divine Female will help you to unlock Emotion in your vessel so that you can be nurtured with Holy Spirit and, in turn, nurture your physical body, mental body, and emotional body.

Your OverSoul is your clearest spiritual guide for your walk home. Ask to see (using your third eye chakra/inner vision) your Divine Mother and Divine Father. They will communicate with you through your intuitive thought and physical sensation. They can help you know when you are sabotaging yourself or neglecting the child within your heart. The more you open to your Divine Male and Divine Female, the faster you clear the old layers of fear's programming, and the easier your evolution on Earth becomes.

An important healing step to bringing in the all-loving, all-powerful and all-knowing Energy of your Divine Male and Divine Female is to clear out old male and old female energy not in balance in your vessel.

CLASS ONE, CLEARING OLD MALE AND OLD FEMALE VISUALIZATION/INTENTION

Imagine you are looking at the front of your body in the mirror. The front and right sides of your vessel are male, and the back and left sides are female.

Now, visualize your front image turning into a great wardrobe filled with many drawers, shelves, and hanging clothes. All the spaces are filled with old male aspects needing to be transformed. Such aspects might include:

giving more than receiving

Ego pride, needing to be better than others

inability to support yourself financially

fears about following your heart where career is concerned

old issues connected with your biological father and other male role models

lying to yourself or others

addictions

shyness and fear of embarrassment

mental illness / obsessive worry / stress

unworthiness / low self-esteem

Ask your little child and your Angels to help you identify what is in the wardrobe that needs to be cleared away.

Imagine you have a fireman's hose hooked up to Violet Fire, God's Energy of Transformation and Forgiveness.

Turn on the hose full-blast, and completely clear out the wardrobe. Say inside, "I Am releasing old male. I Am free."

Walk inside the wardrobe until you see the emerald green Light of your heart chakra.

Ask to meet your Divine Father and merge with His Love and His power.

Ask for His name, and together embrace and merge with God's Child within.

One with your Divine Father and God's Child, imagine you are now looking at the back side of yourself. Clear out the old female wardrobe. Aspects of the old female may be for you:

repressed emotion
denial of feelings
difficulty in setting boundaries and communicating boundaries
denial of physical beauty and sexuality
neediness
giving and receiving out of balance
denial of physical needs / self sacrifice
shortness of breath / exhaustion and physical illness
shame, guilt, unworthiness, and victim-consciousness
infancy and childhood issues with your biological / adoptive mother and other female role models

Turn on your Violet Fire hose and again, clear out all the old female energy in your wardrobe.

Breathe in deeply, and exhale slowly; say inside, "I Am forgiveness."

Now, imagine the child in your heart handing you a ruby pink Light floodlight, and shine the Light into your clean wardrobe.

Watch the Holy Spirit completely redecorate your entire wardrobe, front and back.

Step into the ruby pink Light and ask to meet your Divine Mother.

Ask for Her name and merge with Her, one with your Divine Male and with God's Child.

Say inside, "I Am one with Mother Father God, Divine Love and Creation. I Am the miracle of balance."

We hope you will clean out and organize your wardrobe often. Each time, you will clear more layers of separation between your human soul and your OverSoul. Receive the Divine Love of your OverSoul into your vessel, and free your Divine Male and Divine Female so you can live freely. Free God's innocent Child in your heart by transforming all the layers of fear you experienced in your past. Rebirth your infant, and begin a new life walking in Love.

Rebirth, transform, and balance layer by layer.

Every painful or deceiving experience in your past carries a piece of your soul's energy.

Go find it and set humanity free! Your OverSoul presents you with a treasure hunt to discovering all the riches and joy of the Kingdom of God's great Creation!

We walk beside you.

BOOK SIX

Visiting the Human Soul

HEAVEN

Heaven is a very real place, a place filled with God's Sound and Light, a place where Love is all that exists. Heaven is a vibration, a frequency of Sound and Light much higher than the vibration of Earth. In your human reality exist both Heaven (Divine Love) and Earth. Fear causes the vibration of God's Creation to lower, to feel heavier and more solid, and this is why it appears that Heaven and Earth exist in two different places. We wish to help you understand that Heaven is real. It is possible for you to visit this place called Heaven, and it is possible for you to live in Heaven before you die.

As humanity surrenders fear and negativity to God's transforming Love, humanity's vibration goes up, humanity becomes immune to fear's persuasion, and humanity experiences Divine Love everywhere. Humanity begins to live in Heaven.

Understanding your own soul can assist Us in Our work to set you free.

Your soul is connected to each and every soul in the entire human race, just as each cell in your physical body is connected to all other cells. When cells in your physical body transform into malignant cancer cells, they stop listening to the cells around them. Some of these cells may isolate and form a tumor. Human souls are very much like human cells.

The soul in your human vessel is connected through an umbilical chord of Light and Sound to your OverSoul. The OverSoul is the source of God's Energy that created your human soul. Your OverSoul is your soul's mother and father, and your OverSoul has the ability to heal your soul and every cell in your physical body.

When you use your human mind to activate the connection between your OverSoul and soul, you will bring more of God's Love into your human soul each and every moment. Your OverSoul delights in nurturing you. Because your soul touches all other human souls, as your soul is fed, it becomes easier for all souls to activate their connection with their OverSoul. Eventually, all cancers of human souls and human cells are cured forever.

We are asking for your assistance in accelerating this tremendous healing process!

EARTH

When your OverSoul decides to incarnate on Earth, two sacred Energies are released from Heaven: the Energy creating your soul and the Energy creating the Nature Angel or chi (life force) for your physical body. The Nature Angel knows exactly what genetic coding you need to match your biological family. Your Nature Angel designs your physical temple with perfect accuracy, incorporating all mutations, limitations, and vulnerabilities you need to experience and evolve beyond during your life on Earth.

Inside the cells of your physical body is encoded the complete library of information of Mother Father God's experiment of duality on Earth. All you need to remember about the illusion of fear, as well as how to end separation in your earthly reality, is held within the cells of your body. Inside each cell is a map pointing out exactly where your soul needs to go and what your soul is here to accomplish. The map is always changing as you grow and remember and transform the fears you meet on the path home to God.

As your soul's map changes, you experience more moments of Heaven in your day.

Freedom is the ultimate goal of your soul's evolution of discovery.

Your OverSoul, together with your Guides and Guardian Angels, plan your earthly journey in great and perfect detail. All experiences are designed to help you remember where you come from and where you are going. Your OverSoul makes contracts and agreements for all the souls you will connect with. These contracts are to work synergistically to facilitate the remembering for both of you. Their plans allow for no mistakes, as they are created in Heaven. You will make no mistakes in your life. You will have no accidents, for your OverSoul is always guiding you through fear back to eternal love.

LIFETIME

Your journey is not bound by the limitations of one lifetime. Your soul will return as many times as needed to achieve freedom from fear. We are hopeful you will live this life as if it were your last. We see your soul achieving freedom this life!

More than one visit to Earth has been necessary for you to fully experience how Master Fear tries to control the consciousness of humanity. More than one visit to Earth has been required for you to remember that love always wins over evil. Each human soul has access to the lives of all other souls, so even if you believe this visit is your first, your soul remembers millions. All souls will achieve freedom, and it will feel as if it happens at the same time, during the same life, for all people. We believe the time has come!

DEATH

From Our perspective, humans are dead until they free their minds and bodies of fear. Each time you choose to believe fear has power over you, you are committing suicide. Every moment you choose Love and trust in God's plan, you become more alive. We see you resurrecting your Self from death. We see humanity rising up from the grave of fear and dancing the celebration of life on Earth.

Physical death is another mystery. Is it possible for you live forever in the same physical body? First, We need you to understand what being physical is all about.

Inside your second chakra live your human soul and your Nature Angel. The Nature Angel is responsible for expressing God's Sound and Light in the form of Creation. Creation energy is also called the chi or life force. To hold God's Energy in the form of matter, your Nature Angel lowers the vibration of energy to what humans perceive as solid and tangible. When your physical body has absorbed or experienced all the fear it can hold, the chi burns out, just like a candle.

The OverSoul calls the human soul back to Itself, and your Nature Angel returns to Heaven to create a new body for you. Because this new body exists at Heaven's high vibration of pure Love, it appears you have left the Earth entirely. Your old physical body remains at the vibration of Earth and is recycled back into basic components of physical matter. When your soul returns to Heaven, all of your loving thoughts and feelings of Oneness with other human souls and the Earth, herself, travel with you.

Likewise, all your fearful thoughts and any blocked emotions remain on the Earth. Because your soul is responsible for your whole human vessel, you are given the opportunity to work with your Angels and Guides to clean up any negativity you left behind on the Earth.

We call this your "soul gathering." We hope you will choose to gather all the abandoned thought, emotion, and creation/action energy of your human soul while you are still living on Earth. Again, as you take responsibility for your vessel, you assist all humanity in raising the vibration of Earth to that of Heaven. Heaven is coming closer every day.

As you intend to gather your soul's Light and Sound by transforming the fear in your human vessel, your conscious mind fuses with your higher mind, the mind of your OverSoul. As you allow more love to flow into your vessel, your human soul opens to receiving more and more Sound and Light from your OverSoul. When the OverSoul and human soul unite as one on Earth, the chi can burn forever.

At this moment, you can choose immortality, and you can decide with assistance from your Nature Angel to create a physical body at will, anywhere you like. You can also decide to merge the physical body/creation energy, mental body/thought energy, and emotional body/Holy Spirit Energy back into your spiritual body and again exist as Divine Love, the pure Energy of God's Sound and Light.

Fear creates the illusion of separation between your soul and the OverSoul. Fear causes your vessel to die, and love allows you to live. Be brave enough to know your soul and walk together consciously on your path home to Heaven. *Heaven is life, and We believe now is the moment for humanity to come to life!*

BEING ALIVE

Being truly alive is exactly what you are ascending into. Angels define "ascension" as freedom on Earth. Many human souls have achieved freedom from fear and have evolved into Heaven's vibration. They walk with you on your Earth, touching you, and sending you messages, "Heaven and Earth are united as one."

They say to you, "Trust in God and see the reality of total love." As you continue to take responsibility for transforming your fearful thoughts and reactions into loving thoughts and faith, these ascended souls become part of your conscious reality. An ascended human soul has become a master over fear and is immune from fear's trickery.

EVERY HUMAN SOUL IS AN ASCENDING MASTER. We remind you often, Masters never go backwards on their path home. Help Us help the graduating class of humanity ascend out of Earth's schoolroom of separation into Earth's playground of Love everlasting.

The Twelve Archangels of the Central Soul invite you to attend Our class on soul gathering:

ANGEL HOME-STUDY COURSE FOR ASCENDING MASTERS

CLASS REQUIREMENTS:

Requirements for Our course include the following:

determination to free your human vessel from fear's illusions

courage to follow God's Will, the will of your heart

willingness to take responsibility for creating your outer reality

willingness to transform all negative and fearful thoughts into Love and Oneness

willingness to unlock Holy Spirit and free your emotional body

willingness to learn how to nurture your physical temple and treat your body with love and respect

willingness to trust that God lives in everyone and that all people have equal potential for successfully completing this course

accepting and trusting that all human souls are automatically enrolled in Our home-study course for ascending Masters

(Awareness of what humanity is doing on Earth helps humanity graduate at Godspeed)

Last, visiting your human soul and learning how to love your Self as Mother Father God loves you

CLASS 1, CLEARING UNWORTHINESS FROM THE SECOND (SOUL) CHAKRA Unworthiness is a belief — unconscious, subconscious, and sometimes conscious — that the value of being human is less than being an Angel, less than Mother Father God. With this belief, the human soul remains separate from God, God's Creation, and the Divine Destiny for the human Self.

Held within your soul is tremendous knowledge describing the details of how you are called to break free of fear and fear's illusions. The soul understands it must assist the mental body in clearing away fear's concepts of unworthiness, defeat, inequality, and separation. The soul actively creates with the OverSoul outer- and inner-life challenges to accomplish freedom on all levels.

The second chakra, located just below the navel, supplies Divine Love to both your soul and chi force. Together, the soul and chi give your entire vessel creative, sexual, and life or nurturing forces. These combined forces are called the kundalini. When the soul chakra is blocked by misqualified (low vibration) energy produced from fearful thought (inherited, past life, past, or present), the kundalini energy can short-circuit.

WHEN THE KUNDALINI FORCES ARE DISTURBED, the mental body has great difficulty in transforming fearful, negative, and victim-consciousness thinking. The creative flow of ideas coming through from the higher mind of the OverSoul is continuously interrupted. When this flow is interrupted, it is difficult for the mind to stay focused and identify what actions are needed to manifest the creative ideas.

The emotional body becomes blocked, and the Holy Spirit cannot flow throughout the entire vessel. This can create feelings (messages to the mental body) of depression, hatred of Self and others, deep despair and loneliness and intense isolation from other human beings or nature or both.

If the kundalini energies are short-circuiting in the physical body, the physical body may be attracted to chemical substances, pain, and abusive sexual relations. Blocked kundalini can contribute to slothfulness of the physical self as well as illness.

Disruption of the kundalini flow can contribute to addiction to substances, activities, thought patterns, and relationships to animals, people, and material possessions. One such addiction is that of self-sacrifice and the reverse, unbalanced receiving or greed.

About human sexual relationship, We ask you to remember that when two people are sexual, they are sharing their kundalini. Kundalini is a most powerful and sacred manifestation of Divine Love.

We encourage you to know and Love your whole vessel before you share your soul in sexual exchange with another. It is not enough to love with the mind. Love with your whole vessel, and both partners will benefit greatly from the synergistic sharing of the soul and the chi!

TRANSFORMING UNWORTHINESS AND FREEING THE KUNDALINI

WE ASK YOU TO DO THIS IMAGERY/INTENTION EXERCISE OFTEN UNTIL EVERY HUMAN SOUL IS FREE!*

Lie down, close your eyes, and breathe. Fill your mind with Violet Fire and say softly, "I Am Love."

Invite your Divine Male and Divine Female to open the second chakra.

Empty all that binds your soul with your intention, "I Am Love."

Become one with every gram of unworthiness in your entire vessel.

Say inside, "Unworthiness, come forth into the Light and Sound of God."

*This imagery is included on the audio CD.

Feel the darkness that chokes the sacred kundalini and release it with all the power inside you. Imagine you are filled and surrounded with blazing Violet Fire, then ruby red Holy Spirit, and finally white gold Light of Divine Love.

Say inside, "I Am completely one with Divine Love."

Imagine you are bathing in a beautiful coral, peach Light, the Light of Peace and Serenity. This is the kundalini fire. Move the Light up and down your vessel, out through the soles of your feet, the palms of your hands and the crown of your head. See it pouring out of and into each cell of your body, cleansing fear away from your soul forever.

You may drift off to sleep for a short time while your Over-Soul adjusts your vibration. When you feel complete and ready to rise, say gently, "I Am Love."

CLASS 2, MEETING YOUR NATURE ANGEL AND STRENGTHENING THE CHI Each human vessel provides a home for a Nature Angel, and this Angel provides Creation energy to the human being. We remind you, a human is God's Energy in four aspects: Divine Thought, Divine Emotion, Divine Love, and Creation. Creation energy unifies thought, emotion, and love and generates physical matter, such as stars, planets, human beings, animals, plants, and rocks.

The Nature Angel governs the chi or life force energy for your physical body. When you respect your body as God's great Creation, your Nature Angel allows the flow of the chi to increase. Your body needs to move, dance, exercise, and be touched by human beings. Asking your Nature Angel to teach you Creation's way of nurturing your body helps the life force to flow and makes moving, dancing, and exercising effortless. Your Nature Angel is willing to help you be a true disciple of treating your physical body as a precious temple containing God's Divine Love.

Inside you lives God's Child, and the child must play and receive physical affection. You can do this by massaging your own body and welcoming affection from people and Angels you trust. We present you with how your Nature Angel can help you take better care of your physical temple and bring you eternal youth. As you nurture and exercise the muscles of God's house, you help clear the second chakra of misqualified kundalini. God's Child knows your Nature Angel, and God's Child understands the soul. Allow this child to play, and increase the flow of the chi so the sacred kundalini can keep you human, fully God, and God fully human.

COMMUNICATING WITH YOUR NATURE ANGEL*

Close your eyes, breathe air deep into your abdomen, and exhale completely. Continue to focus on your breathing.

Place your hands on your second chakra, just below the navel, and imagine finding a door underneath your hands. Ask the child of your heart for the key to open this magic door.

Keep your hands on your second chakra, and now imagine that you and God's Child are walking through the sacred door. Say inside or out loud, "I Am here to meet my life force."

It is not important whether you actually see your Nature Angel. Trust that you will see the chi in time, or feel this Angel, or both. Send love to your Nature Angel, and allow the love to multiply and flow back.

Ask your Angel to assist you in taking excellent care of your physical body. Remember to ask for your Angel's name so you can call on him or her to help you exercise effortlessly and stay disciplined. Ask that all the food you eat be filled with health and love. Ask your Angel to let any food your body doesn't need to pass on through so that you metabolize only what is for your vessel's greatest good and highest joy.

---

*This imagery is included on the audio CD.

Listen for guidance from your Nature Angel on any health concerns you have.

Say inside, "I Am life force, free and immortal." Your Nature Angel is your own personal trainer, nutritionist, and whole-body healer, all in one.

Many healers of the physical body are available to you, and We are hopeful you will remember to check in with your own internal expert to ensure you are receiving the best type of assistance for *your* body.

CLASS 3, ONENESS* *As your OverSoul fuses with your soul and your soul assists your physical, mental, and emotional bodies to resurrect from death, all the Earth rejoices. Because of your faith and courage, you help all people to live free of fear.*

As your OverSoul fuses with your soul and your soul and Nature Angel send forth the sacred kundalini, all the Earth celebrates. Because of your *discipline and love, you help* all *people create a new human body. This human body is free of disease, free of cancer, and free of death.*

---

*This imagery is included on the audio CD.

As your OverSoul fuses with your soul and your soul connects with God's Child in your heart, God in four aspects is completely unified within your human vessel. Because of your will to transform your thoughts into Divine Thought, your feelings into Divine Emotion, your action into Divine Love and your physical body into God's temple, you bring Heaven and Earth together.

As your OverSoul fuses with your soul, you consciously begin to connect with all people and all Mother Father God's Creation. Because of the Oneness inside of you, you create Oneness and all the blessings of Heaven in all your experiences. You experience Love with every breath; in every moment, you live in joy.

Welcome to Heaven!

It is the Will of God for humanity to remember God is a most magnificent spiral of Sound and Light, a symphony playing joyful music, and your soul is a most critical instrument in the orchestra!

Welcome Home!

We invite you to listen to the meditation called, "Rainbow Soul" on the audio CD.

Angel Letters

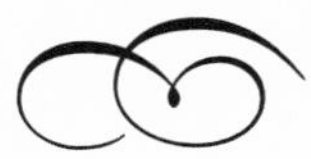

COMMUNICATION

Dear Humanity,

Human beings seek independence of thought, word, and action and, therefore, usually do not enjoy being told what to think, say, feel, or do. The Ego has developed strong protection devices so that even the most heartfelt advice offered by another often falls on deaf ears.

I Am Archangel Gabriel, Kingdom of Communication, and I Am presenting you with a method to communicate your deepest concern for another without interfering in their evolution and their destiny. We call this Our *Angel Airwave*, and We promise miraculous results for the greatest benefit for all concerned.

The Angel Airwave sends your message through thought and emotion to the person with whom you need to communicate. The receiver hears the message as if that person thought of the idea or revelation on his or her own. Human beings don't "get it" until they "know it" for their Selves. You and the child of your heart can relax, for you know you have "said" what you need to say. The receiver of your message receives the transmission in God's time according to God's Will.

Here is how it works.

Call on Gabriel to open the channel between your OverSoul and the OverSoul of the person with whom you wish to communicate.

Think what you wish to tell the person, don't worry about the words or if the message is too harsh or too gentle, just *say it*. Open your heart and send love, yes, even if you are completely exasperated with whom you are thinking about.

Gabriel will transmute all negative energy connected with the message, using God's Violet Fire of Transformation and Forgiveness. Know that your message will be sent at just the best moment and will be received just at the peak of the receiver's awareness.

Listen to your intuition, for often you will hear a reply, and you will always receive confirmation from Gabriel that your message was both sent and received, according to God's Will, for the greatest good of all.

Express yourself! Don't hold back! Communicate in a way that works, a way in which you can be heard!

I Am one with you always! Love, Gabe

LETTER FROM THE TWELVE ARCHANGEL KINGDOMS

Children and Their Guardian Angels

Dear Humanity,

It is easier for newly born infants to see their Guardian Angels than it is for them to see anything in physical form on Earth. Their Angels play with them and surround them in God's Love. Their Guardian Angels help their soul to make the transition in vibration between Heaven and Earth and adjust to being in a tiny body. Babies sleep so they can grow, and they sleep so their Angels can help them adjust to their new environment, an environment where fear's shabungi is still present.

As the infant grows into a toddler, his or her Guardian Angel is just as present, although now the baby is more distracted by what is happening in the physical world. Babies must learn how to communicate again with spoken words instead of just communicating with thought and Heaven's music.

The toddler and preschooler can still see and feel their Angels with ease and often address them as invisible playmates. These playmates do not break things or say anything hurtful. The child's Ego is attempting to create separation and already trying out control and avoiding responsibility. The Guardian Angels are not allowed to interfere in the separation because the soul has come to experience fear and then transmute it in life.

The more imaginative the child stays, the more real and alive the child's Guardian Angels stay. We are hopeful you will encourage your children to keep their imagination open!

Ask your children about their Angels, and they will tell you all about their friends of Light and Sound. Encourage them to call on their Guardian Angels for assistance and for entertainment when bored or lonely.

Here is an exercise you can do together with your young child or teen:

Sit together in a comfortable room. Have soothing, enjoyable music softly playing in the background.

Close your eyes, and both (or all) of you imagine you are sitting in a giant bubble of pink Light. Breathe, and welcome your Guardian Angels to come and tell you their names.

What colors are they wearing, and what do they look like? Remember they may look different from what you might expect.

Ask them anything you like. When you are ready, open your eyes, and share your experiences with each other.

Call on your Guardian Angels for all things great and small. Nothing is too big or too little to ask your Angel to help you with.

Angels always follow God's Law of One. This means We will only do what is for the greatest joy and good of all people and all God's Creation.

We are real! We are all around you! Call out to Us and know Mother Father God loves you always!

Love and Joy to you,

The Twelve Archangel Kingdoms of the Central Soul

P.S. Dear Parents,

Guardian Angels are most loving counselors. Remind your children to call on their Angels for any tragic event such as the loss of a pet or loved one. Angels can assist in calming and reassuring your child during times of stress for the family and during major transitions. Send your child's Guardian Angels to school each day. Remember, your child's soul does know what it must experience, and Angels can help these lessons come and go with clarity and ease.

LETTER FROM THE TWELVE ARCHANGEL KINGDOMS

Angels Speak on Crisis Management

For any crisis or stressful situation, We recommend the following:

Breathe.

Call on your Angels or say, "I surrender."

Breathe.

Tell your Angels exactly what you need in the present moment, and be as specific as you possibly can.

Breathe.

Keep your mind on the present and say, "I Am calling on the Will of God."

Breathe and trust all is in Divine Order. We are with you! *We are with you always!*

After the crisis is over, sit or lie down and ask your Angels, Divine Male, Divine Female, and God's Child inside your heart, "Why did I create this, and what do I need to discover about myself here in this situation?"

Breathe and observe. Fear can teach you much about your Self and where you give your power away. Remember Master Fear is actually an Angel in disguise. Fear gives you an opportunity to trust in God with all your vessel.

CRISIS MANAGEMENT TECHNIQUES FOR THOSE WHO HELP OTHERS IN CRISIS: Before you pick up the telephone or open your office door, breathe and say inside, "I Am one with God." Surround your Self with white gold Light of Divine Love and Protection.

Immediately ask Us to send God's Light and Sound to the person in need.

Listen for where the person is caught in fear, and call on Archangel Michael to help the person see the Truth.

Maintain a sacred space for your Self and remember not to get enticed into the other person's drama. Every experience is created by the OverSoul to help the human soul evolve.

Tell Us exactly how you perceive the situation from your human perspective, and tell Us how We can help your client, friend, or loved one. Do not be afraid to boss Us around and tell Us what to do. Trust all is in Divine Order. We will respond immediately, if not sooner, to all requests!

Miracles are everywhere you look for them, and miracles happen in abundance.

As you see miracles manifest in crisis, your faith grows. Ask for experiences to help your faith grow without crisis. You are the creator of your reality. If you can transform fear into love without experiencing fear, go for it! Fear is a magnificent tool for building trust and faith in God. Remember, it is only a tool, and often Divine Love can work just as well, if not better, for building trust and faith in God. When you take God's Love and Oneness for granted, be sure fear is around the corner to help you learn a bit more about the infinite power of God.

LETTER FROM THE TWELVE ARCHANGELS

DEPRESSION AND PAIN

Human beings can become most uncomfortable when they do not receive what they hope for at the time they want their desire to manifest. Depression usually happens when humans feel hopeless because their life seems to be staying in the same stagnant experience.

We present you with Our home remedy for alleviating discomfort and dissatisfaction. We hope you enjoy this short imagery meditation and healing music recorded on the *Angels Guide* audio CD located in the sleeve on the inside back cover of the book.

THE EXERCISE*

Close your eyes and imagine you are resting in the loving arms of your Angel

Breathe in immortal love

Breathe in hope and demand God's Divine rescue

Surrender to your discomfort

Know it is almost over

Yell and scream and blow up your life in God's Violet Fire of Transformation

It is almost over, this discomfort

Know you are clearing pain and unhappiness for all people everywhere

Know it is leaving and you are learning and remembering with each painful feeling

God is REAL and You are one with God

Ask Us to help you see the Light at the end of the tunnel of your depression

Hold My Hand for I Am always with you

Today is a good day for a miracle!

---

*This imagery is included on the audio CD.

The Archangels Glossary

ANGEL Being of pure Divine Love whose purpose is to nurture and assist, obeying The Law of One (for the greatest good of all concerned).

ARCHANGEL Messenger for God's Will assigned the task of bringing the human race home to the heart of Mother Father God. Archangels are protectors and guides for all healers called to assist others or called to heal Mother Earth.

AURA Radiating energy field surrounding each body (spiritual, mental, emotional, and physical) of the vessel. The aura's colors give information on the health status of each body. The aura colors of the spiritual body give information on the life purpose and God service of the human being.

BODY OF LIGHT AND SOUND Spiritual body vibrating at the frequency of pure love (no fear). The Body of Light and Sound consists of God's Energy from the Center of God. Also called the OverSoul.

CENTER The still, quiet, and satisfied place inside the mind and heart. The Center is the home of God within the human vessel, and it is the place of feeling content and united with all of God's Creation. In the Center, the mind can open and connect with the intuition and personal Truth.

CENTRAL SOUL (SUN) The center point of the heart of Mother Father God, Divine Love, and Creation. This is sacred space where Mother Father God births each particle of God's Energy, making up the formed Cosmos.

CHAKRA Energy center supplying God's Divine Love to the spiritual, mental, emotional, and physical bodies. Chakras work like automobile batteries in that they need to be fully charged and well connected to the vessel. Each chakra has a different target of where to send God's Light and Sound.

CHI The life force energy generated by the Nature Angel to create and nourish the physical body.

CHILD OF GOD The all-believing, all-trusting, totally free, and beautiful child inside your heart. God's Child brings in Divine Love from the OverSoul and gives love to the Ego Self and Shadow Self, as well as the mental, emotional, and physical bodies.

COSMOS All of Mother Father God's Creation, unformed, forming, formed and recycling.

CREATION God's Energy in Light and Sound vibrating at a frequency where the perceiver sees the energy as tangible with taste, touch, feel, audible sound, sight or knowing. Mother Earth and all her inhabitants are examples of Creation.

DEVA An Angel who designs physical creation and lowers the vibration of God's Energy to achieve manifestation of the physical form. Devas design planets and human bodies and all that is physical.

DIVINE The Truth and Love and Will of Mother Father God resonating at the highest and purest vibration of Sound and Light.

DIVINE GRACE An unexpected gift of insight, forgiveness, or understanding. Grace is Mother Father God's way of showing affection.

DIVINE DESTINY The ultimate fulfillment of living life from the Center. Destiny is equal to achieving Oneness and transforming karmic debt. this has to do with the freedom of knowing who you are and what your purpose is on Earth.

DIVINE LAW God's laws supercede all human law. Divine justice serves from the Center of God and always manifests according to God's Will and for the highest joy and greatest good of the Cosmos.

DIVINE LOVE The vibration of all of God's Energy. Divine Love is the expression of Oneness with all Divine Thought, Emotion, and Creation. Divine Love is God, and God is Divine Love.

DIVINE ORDER Mother Father God's plan for the Earth and Cosmos perfectly orchestrated by God's Will in God's time. All events in Earth's history have unfolded according to Divine Order. It is Divine Order for Earth and Heaven to be One.

DUALITY The separation of human thought, emotion, and creation from Oneness with God. Duality creates the illusion of fear in opposition to the Truth of Divine Love.

EARTH A manifestation of God's Creation existing at the present moment. Planet Earth is the schoolroom for all souls needing to experience duality for their evolution. Planet Earth's vibration, because of fearful thoughts, is lower (less pure) than the vibration of Heaven. Earth's vibration is purified constantly and is rapidly returning to the vibration of Divine Love.

EGO The part of the human mind — unconscious, subconscious, and conscious — believing in fear. Usually, thoughts generated by the Ego mind are conscious. The Ego defines the human personality in relationship to other people and the surrounding world.

EMOTION Mother God's Holy Spirit giving the power to manifest Divine Thought on Earth.

EMOTIONAL BODY The heart Center and the place where Oneness within the human Self, as well as with all God's Creation, is experienced.

ENERGY Light and Sound, Mother Father God's Energy one with Divine Love. Energy creates all God's great Cosmos, formed and unformed. The word "energy" is sometimes used to mean a function or direction of God's Divine Love. Healing energy is an example of God's Energy having a specific purpose and direction.

EVOLUTION The continuous learning and breaking out of fearful thought. Evolution is the process of returning the human vessel back to the vibration and consciousness of Heaven.

FAITH The opposite of control. A sincere intention to trust in Mother Father God's Divine plan and an ever-deepening knowing that true Love is all there is.

FATE The culmination of experiences designed by the OverSoul to assist the human soul in breaking out of fear's illusions, conceptions, and limitations.

FATHER GOD The masculine aspect of God, which generates Light and Divine Thought Energy.

FEAR Deceptive and misqualified human thought-energy, creating the illusion that humans are separate from God.

FEELING Messages from the mental body or from the spiritual body to the mental body describing where Holy Spirit/emotion is blocked, or flowing, in the human vessel.

GOD All there is and all there ever shall be. God is Energy, and this Energy is both Light and Sound. God's Light and Sound generate Divine Love, and Divine Love creates God's Creation.

GREATEST GOOD Benefits the entire Cosmos as well as all human beings, nature, and the evolution of all human souls.

GUIDE A Loving Being working together with the OverSoul to offer reassurance and direction to the soul traveling on Earth.

HEALING The clearing of fear from some part of the human vessel.

HEAVEN A reality where fear does not exist. Heaven is the vibration of Oneness and pure Divine Love, the sacred place where Earth is traveling to.

HIGHEST JOY The most all-encompassing and euphoric joy expressed by the heart Center. Highest joy is experienced when human beings are united with Mother Father God's Divine Love.

HOLY SPIRIT Mother God's Sound in the form of Divine Emotion. Red Fire of God's Divine Love in all shades of red and pink, bringing unconditional love, compassion, and freedom.

HOME The heart center when the human Ego mind is quiet and the human vessel feels completely united with mind, heart, body, and soul. Home also means experiencing the vibration of Heaven and Oneness with all of God's Creation.

HUMAN BEING A Child of God deserving Oneness.

I AM The Center of the heart of God where all of God's Creation is one, the Central Soul, and the origin of all that is formed and unformed. "I Am" defines the human Center and is the alpha and omega of God's Energy.

IMAGINATION The doorway to experiencing spiritual clairvoyance and receiving and sending visual messages to God and to God's Creation.

INNER CHILD God's Child wrapped in all the human experiences creating the illusion of abandonment by Mother Father God during this lifetime on Earth.

INTUITION Knowing, sensing, visual, or auditory messages coming from the spiritual body usually to the mental body, and sometimes to the emotional and/or physical Body.

KARMA Incomplete lessons from schoolroom Earth that must be balanced for the soul to continue evolving into a state of Oneness with all Creation.

KUNDALINI The combined and integrated energies of the fire of the soul together with the chi or life force. As the human evolves, the force of the kundalini connects directly with the Light and Sound of the OverSoul.

LAW OF ONE The law stating that all God's Children are influenced by the thoughts, feelings, and actions of all people. If any particles of God's Energy are harmed or vibrating at a frequency less than Divine Love, all of God experiences this disharmony. When the Law of One is enacted, God's Energy is rebalanced in a way that is for the greatest good of all. When any human helps himself or herself to evolve and trust in God's Love, all humanity benefits.

LIFE FORCE The chi energy produced by the Nature Angel of the human vessel which gives life to all the cells of the physical body.

LIGHT Divine Thought, Mother Father God's Divine Love directed for the purpose of healing human consciousness, both individual and global.

LUCIFER MICHAEL Archangel Kingdom of God's united Light and Willpower. The Archangel Lucifer Michael split into two Angelic Kingdoms in order to create the illusion of separation and fear on planet Earth.

MANIFESTATION The final step in the process of Creation on Earth. Bringing a creative idea to fruition, or the actual fulfillment of experiencing a miracle. Manifestation of money would be the moment the actual physical money is in sight.

MASTER A being totally connected with the spiritual Self and living free of fear in the mental, emotional and physical bodies.

MENTAL BODY The body of the vessel creating and receiving thought.

MICHAEL'S FIRE The energy produced by the Will (throat) chakra fused with God's Energy of Truth and Awareness. Michael's Flame burns through deception and karmic debt.

MIRACLE A magical moment of awareness of receiving and/or experiencing exactly what is needed for the greatest good of all concerned.

MOTHER GOD The female aspect of God generating Sound and Divine Emotion. Mother God's Energy is Holy Spirit, the Fire of unconditional Love and Compassion for all God's Creation. Mother Earth is a representative (Angel) of Mother God.

MUSIC The most potent healing energy of the Cosmos. Angels can best be defined as Divine Music. God's Divine Music is both Sound and Light delivered at the vibration of Oneness.

ONE To be completely united with on all levels of consciousness and energy.

OVERSOUL The spiritual body of the human vessel still remaining inside of Oneness and the vibration of Heaven. The OverSoul is the Higher Self or Intuitive Mind directing the soul in the human vessel on the evolutionary path home to God.

PHYSICAL BODY Temple of God's Love holding the precious human being's thought and emotion. The physical body is the container existing at the densest vibration of God's Energy on Earth and the body requiring the highest quality and quantity of God's Energy for complete healing.

RESURRECTION Rebirth from fear's illusions of mortality of mind, heart, body, and soul. Resurrection is achieving a new level of awareness of Oneness with God.

SEPARATION A belief that fear is real and has power over the Divine Destiny of the human vessel. Separation is the illusion that human beings are disconnected from Mother Father God and that Creation is disconnected or apart from Divine Love.

SHADOW Misqualified thought energy generated from fear, which creates separation between the Ego Self and the God Self. The Shadow is the deceptive, self-sabotaging, and fearful aspect of the Ego that often remains hidden until the mental Self opens and begins the process of healing. Violet Fire transforms the Shadow Self into the God Self.

SOUL Emissary of the OverSoul incarnating on Earth to heal karma and transform fear back into love.

SOUND Divine Emotion generating an all-powerful, all-loving clearing and healing force required for human evolution and freedom. God's Sound and Light are always fused and create Holy Spirit, the Fire of Mother God's unconditional Love.

SPIRITUAL BODY Body of Sound and Light uniting the OverSoul with the soul. The spiritual body houses the chakras and provides all healing energies needed to achieve complete freedom of the human vessel on Earth.

THIRD EYE Energy center/chakra located in the center of the brain, which is responsible for receiving and sending all intuitive communication.

THOUGHT The male aspect of God's Energy allowing for the conception of all Creation. Thought is the universal communicator between all particles of God's Energy.

TONING The audible or silent action of expressing God's Sound to help clear fear or negative energy from the vessel.

TRANSFORMATION Alchemical process of raising the vibration of thought to a higher level of love. The experience of changing fear into love and death into life. Divine Transformation can only be used to achieve greater awareness and freedom from fear and fear's illusions.

TRUST Intention and allowing the mind to believe that unconditional and constant support from Mother Father God is the only true reality for the human being.

TRUTH Oneness with God.

TWELVE ARCHANGELS OF THE CENTRAL SOUL (SUN) Musical instruments of Mother Father God's Energy holding the vision of humanity's freedom from Master Fear.

VESSEL The energy field or protecting aura holding God's Energy of Creation in a physical body that appears to be solid and finite.

VICTIM-CONSCIOUSNESS Conscious, subconscious, or unconscious belief in abandonment by Mother Father God, another human being, or Mother Earth. The refusal to take responsibility for creating one's own reality on Earth and the belief that this reality is unchangeable.

VIOLET FIRE Light and Sound generated by the crown chakra, catalyzing transformation of fearful thought into loving thought.

VISUALIZATION The action of creating a mental image of the Self, another person, or an experience for the purpose of healing the vessel.

WILL Mother Father God's Divine plan to bring all humanity back to a state of Oneness with God. Will is the manifestation of inner strength to trust in God and transform fear back into Love.

WHITE GOLD LIGHT The Light and Sound of Divine Love. White gold Light is often called the Christ-Buddha Energy.

WHITE LIGHT BROTHERHOOD/SISTERHOOD All-knowing and all-loving Ascended Masters having lived or living on Earth and experiencing all races and economic and religious backgrounds known to humankind. Beings of God's Light and Sound having achieved Oneness with God and all God's Creation with the entire human vessel. The Faculty of Earth's School of Ending Separation.

AVAILABLE FALL 1998

You've heard a sampling of the music from **ANGELS GUIDE** on the CD in the back of this book, now enjoy more *Angels Guide*.

ANGELS GUIDE SOUNDTRACK features full instumental versions of the music from *Angels Guide*. (CD, cassette)

THE MESSAGES AUDIOBOOK features all 36 messages read by the author with music. (2-CD, 2-cassette)

THE TREASURY AUDIOBOOK features all six "books" of the Angel Treasury and the four Angel letters read by the author with music. (2-CD, 2-cassette)

THE MEDITATIONS six meditations with music, led by Belinda Womack, to complement the *Angel Treasury*. (CD, cassette)

THE CD-ROM provides almost 200 pages of new material in an interactive format. Ask for Angelic Guidance from over a hundred areas: family issues including conflict resolution, addictions and co-dependency, friendship issues; romantic and romantic partner issues, career, finances, life transitions, wellness and self-esteem.

Available everywhere!

Previews and Belinda Womack's workshop and event schedule are on the web site: **www.angelsguide.com**

Direct order line: 1-800-525-4274

ANGELS GUIDE AUDIO CD

INCLUDED IN THE BACK OF THIS BOOK

The Audio CD in the back of your book has 73 minutes of new music with the voice of Belinda Womack. There are readings and visualizations from the book, as well as a guided meditation, all created under her supervision. Included are:

BOOK 1: Where Does God Come From? *20:44*

MESSAGE 1: The Holy Spirit *2:31*

MESSAGE 8: How to Love a Human Being *4:01*

MESSAGE 15: Facing Your Shadow Self *3:25*

MESSAGE 36: The Law of Attraction *3:21*

BOOK 2 STEP 1: Filling the Vessel with Divine Love *1:55*

BOOK 3 IMAGERY: Angel Keys to Freedom of the Human Vessel *4:02*

BOOK 5 IMAGERY: Visualization on Rebirthing *3:00*

BOOK 5 IMAGERY: Intention for Freeing God's Child *4:45*

BOOK 6 IMAGERY: Transforming Unworthiness *3:07*

BOOK 6 IMAGERY: Communicating with your Nature Angel *2:44*

BOOK 6: Class 3, Oneness *2:51*

LETTER FOUR: Depression and Pain *2:10*

RAINBOW SOUL: A Guided Meditation *13:40*

Angels Guide Music is composed and produced by Robert Davidson, Angel Messages music is composed by Daniel Cowett, arranged by Daniel Cowett and Robert Davidson, produced by Robert Davidson. For more information on *Angels Guide Music* check the web site: www.angelsguide.com, call 1 800-525-4274, or write to Angels Guide Music, P.O. Box 0260, Tappan, NY 10983-0260.